Unlock the Door

Write the correct answers.

1. Write the numerals in standard form.

   sixty-eight thousand, six _____

   eighteen thousand, four hundred ten _____

   one hundred eighty-nine thousand, three hundred fifty-two _____

   one million, seven thousand, nine hundred two _____

2. Write the numerals as decimals.

   four and two tenths _____

   twelve and seven tenths _____

   five and three tenths _____

3. Write the numerals in word form.

   2,003 _____

   1,423,703 _____

   45,305 _____

   54.4 _____

   81.9 _____

4. Read the expanded form, then write the standard form of the numeral.

   4,000 + 700 + 10 + 3 _____   10,000 + 6,000 + 900 + 20 + 3 _____

   5,000 + 200 + 40 + 9 _____   1,000,000 + 50,000 + 80 + 7 _____

5. Mark an **X** on the hundreds place, circle the tens place, and draw a box
   around the tenths place in each numeral.

   1,286.7   85,203.1   544.91   3,988.5

6. Mark an **X** on the millions place, circle the thousands place, and draw a box
   around the hundredths place in each numeral.

   2,533,742.49   43,100,009.87   7,359,529.23   3,584,239.05

Field Day Fun

Write the value of the underlined digit.

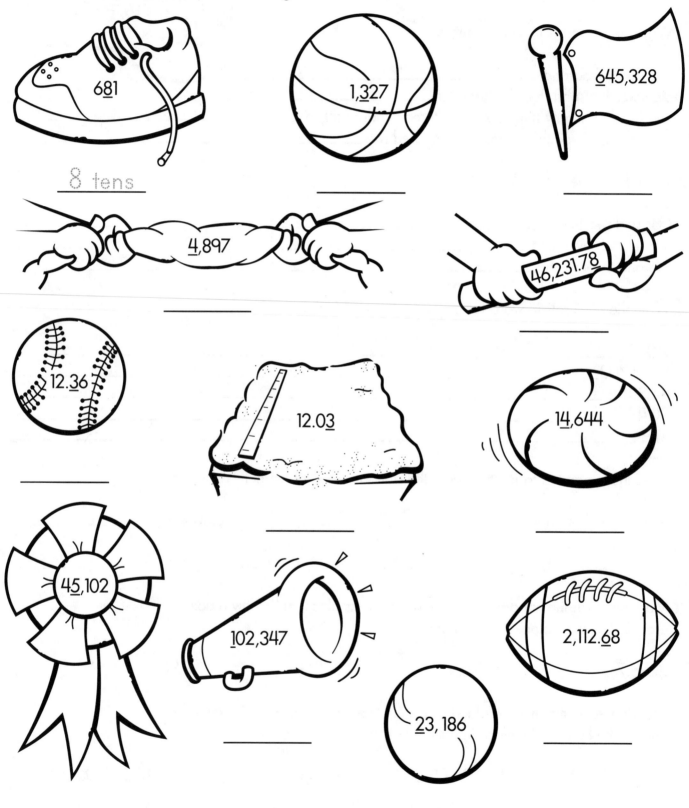

68<u>1</u>

8 tens

1,3<u>2</u>7

<u>6</u>45,328

4,<u>8</u>97

46,231.7<u>8</u>

12.3<u>6</u>

12.0<u>3</u>

1<u>4</u>,644

<u>4</u>5,102

<u>1</u>02,347

2,112.<u>6</u>8

<u>2</u>3,186

Reviewing place value

Your Future is Bright!

Write the correct answers.

1. Round the following numerals to the nearest ten.

527 _____   104 _____   955 _____   423 _____

2. Round the following numerals to the nearest hundred.

689 _____   527 _____   1,365 _____   421 _____

3. Round the following numerals to the nearest thousand.

1,365 _____   1,748 _____   5,231 _____   4,522 _____

4. Round the following numerals to the nearest tenth.

527.63 _____   289.34 _____   671.57 _____   15.85 _____

5. Estimate each sum or difference by rounding each numeral to the nearest hundred.

17,684 + 35,419	+ ___	4,930 + 9,407	+ ___	26,490 + 5,601	+ ___	53,620 + 14,760	+ ___
98,601 − 16,519	− ___	13,481 − 4,681	− ___	47,486 − 29,581	− ___	76,407 − 35,616	− ___

6. Estimate each sum or difference by rounding each numeral to the nearest thousand.

98,753 + 18,491	+ ___	79,254 + 43,601	+ ___	55,760 + 41,632	+ ___	71,487 + 26,418	+ ___
54,307 − 30,817	− ___	92,471 − 45,981	− ___	82,386 − 19,470	− ___	19,491 − 5,691	− ___

Let it shine!

Building Blocks

You need a good foundation!

Solve. Watch the symbols.

578 + 105	85 + 79	174 − 89	1,586 − 1,391	12,211 + 4,657	579 476 + 307
654 321 + 276	54,253 − 1,956	452 − 148	8,645 − 3,794	8,970 + 3,094	6,004 − 3,279
$62.20 + 3.57	$147.38 − 52.02	$38.00 − 9.00	$657.12 + 896.33	5,073 − 1,994	709 + 438
2,234 + 791	6,371 + 1,497	8,419 − 3,791	5,641 − 3,499	2,344 + 9,881	741 + 1,490

Solve.

$(24 - 15) + 7 =$ _____ $17 + (4 \times 9) =$ _____ $23 - (4 \times 5) =$ _____

$(5 + 4) + 6 = (6 + 4) +$ _____ $(7 \times 3) + 8 =$ ___ $+ (4 \times 6)$ $(8 \times 6) + 5 =$ _____

$7 + (2 - 1) = 4 + (3 +$ ___ $)$ $(9 \times 4) - 18 = 28 - (5 \times$ ___ $)$ $(42 - 15) + 9 =$ _____

$(10 -$ ___ $) + 2 = (6 + 3) - 6$ $14 + (7 \times 6) =$ _____ $13 + (8 \times 5) =$ _____

Reviewing addition and subtraction and order of operations

Just Posted!

Solve. Show your work.

Give it a try!

378 x 75	642 x 89	501 x 7	18 x 29	410 x 397

$5\overline{)635}$ $4\overline{)624}$ $8\overline{)230}$ $5\overline{)275}$ $7\overline{)301}$ $2\overline{)309}$

89 x 72	46 x 23	223 x 30	317 x 614	536 x 12	62 x 24

Solve each problem using mental math.

42 x 10 = _____   100 x 23 = _____   10 x 10 = _____   25 x 3 = _____   200 x 4 = _____

What is the average of 12, 5, 9, and 10?

First, add the numerals.
```
  12
  10
   5
+  9
  36
```

Then divide the sum by the number of addends.

$4\overline{)36}$ → 9

The average is 9!

Find the average of each set of numbers.

27, 18, 20, 15   25, 63, 45, 27   25, 86, 92, 75, 62

Massive Amounts of Measuring

Match each object to its correct measurement.

eyedropper	liter	bowl of soup	quart
carton of milk	gram	punch bowl	gallon
paper clip	milliliter	bucket of paint	pint

Ready to measure!

Circle the correct answer.

1. How many inches is 6 feet 9 inches?

   a. 86   b. 81   c. 89   d. 90

2. How many feet are there in one yard?

   a. 3   b. 30   c. 100   d. 10

3. When you are converting larger units to smaller units you?

   a. divide   b. multiply   c. add   d. subtract

4. When you are converting smaller units to larger units you?

   a. divide   b. multiply   c. add   d. subtract

Draw the following.

a line that is 5 centimeters long	a square measuring $1\frac{1}{2}$ inches on all sides
a line that is 3 and $\frac{1}{4}$ inches long	

Reviewing metric and customary units of measure

Parts of the Whole

1. Simplify the fractions.

$\frac{9}{15} =$ $\frac{8}{24} =$ $\frac{5}{40} =$ $\frac{7}{49} =$

$\frac{4}{32} =$ $\frac{8}{48} =$ $\frac{3}{18} =$ $\frac{9}{54} =$

$\frac{8}{56} =$ $\frac{7}{35} =$ $\frac{4}{20} =$ $\frac{3}{21} =$

$\frac{6}{36} =$ $\frac{5}{30} =$ $\frac{3}{27} =$ $\frac{9}{81} =$

2. Write each mixed numeral as an improper fraction.

$5\frac{4}{7} =$ $3\frac{1}{2} =$ $8\frac{3}{4} =$ $4\frac{2}{7} =$

$3\frac{7}{8} =$ $6\frac{2}{3} =$ $1\frac{4}{7} =$ $5\frac{4}{9} =$

$7\frac{2}{9} =$ $3\frac{4}{6} =$ $8\frac{2}{7} =$ $3\frac{8}{9} =$

$2\frac{4}{8} =$ $4\frac{5}{7} =$ $3\frac{2}{3} =$ $4\frac{1}{9} =$

3. Write each improper fraction as a mixed numeral.

$\frac{12}{8} =$ $\frac{14}{6} =$ $\frac{13}{6} =$ $\frac{21}{4} =$

$\frac{18}{5} =$ $\frac{25}{6} =$ $\frac{17}{3} =$ $\frac{23}{7} =$

$\frac{17}{8} =$ $\frac{31}{6} =$ $\frac{28}{9} =$ $\frac{34}{5} =$

$\frac{29}{4} =$ $\frac{28}{7} =$ $\frac{13}{2} =$ $\frac{41}{8} =$

4. Add or subtract, then simplify each sum or difference. Watch the symbols!

$\frac{3}{5} + \frac{1}{5} =$ $\frac{9}{12} + \frac{2}{12} =$ $\frac{10}{13} - \frac{6}{13} =$

$\frac{14}{18} - \frac{4}{18} =$ $\frac{15}{21} - \frac{8}{21} =$ $\frac{5}{12} + \frac{4}{12} =$

$\frac{11}{15} - \frac{9}{15} =$ $\frac{7}{24} + \frac{5}{24} =$ $\frac{7}{11} + \frac{3}{11} =$

$\frac{4}{24} + \frac{4}{24} =$ $\frac{9}{24} - \frac{3}{24} =$ $\frac{12}{32} + \frac{4}{32} =$

Graduated Amounts

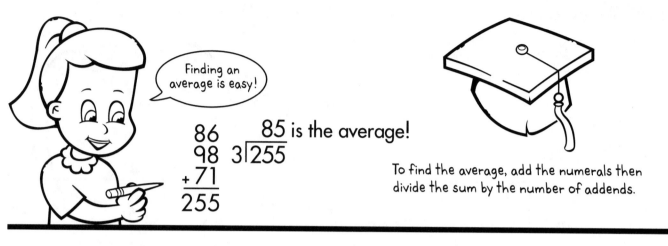

Finding an average is easy!

$$86$$
$$98$$
$$+71$$
$$255$$

$$3\overline{)255}$$ **85** is the average!

To find the average, add the numerals then divide the sum by the number of addends.

Student	Average
Sue D.	94.6
Diane W.	94.7
Clay D.	98.5
Bill R.	95.1
Kelly F.	98.9
Ken M.	90.6

The table shows the class averages of high school seniors.

Put the averages in order from greatest to least.

If a seventh student were added to the list with an average of 90.9, where would his or her average be placed in the order?

Find the total average of the students.

Find the average of both of the girls' scores.

Who has the higher average?

How much of a difference is there between the averages?

Ruthie's math scores:
95, 83, 79, 97, 96, 91, 89, 90
Jean's math scores:
87, 78, 91, 99, 84, 91, 89, 100

Sarah works at a café in the village. Below are her tip totals for the past five days. Find the average.

$10 $14 $13 $18 $20

Look at the point amounts Chris scored during the past season's basketball games. Find the average of his points per game.

24   32   27   40   18   33

Compare it with his 34.7 average from the year before. What is the difference? Did Chris improve or not?

Averaging and comparing numbers

What's the Secret Message?

Multiply. Then write the letter next to each product on the correct lines below to reveal the secret message. Not all letters will be used.

63 x 4 **D**	22 x 3 **S**	50 x 6 **O**	78 x 7 **!**
50 x 2 **K**	36 x 9 **I**	92 x 3 **U**	24 x 5 **D**
85 x 5 **I**	97 x 8 **Y**	47 x 6 **T**	38 x 6 **M**

776   300   276   120   324   252   425   282   546

Blooming Products

Multiply. Then use the code to color the picture.

Color Code:

Purple	Green	Yellow
under 599	600 to 2,000	over 2,000

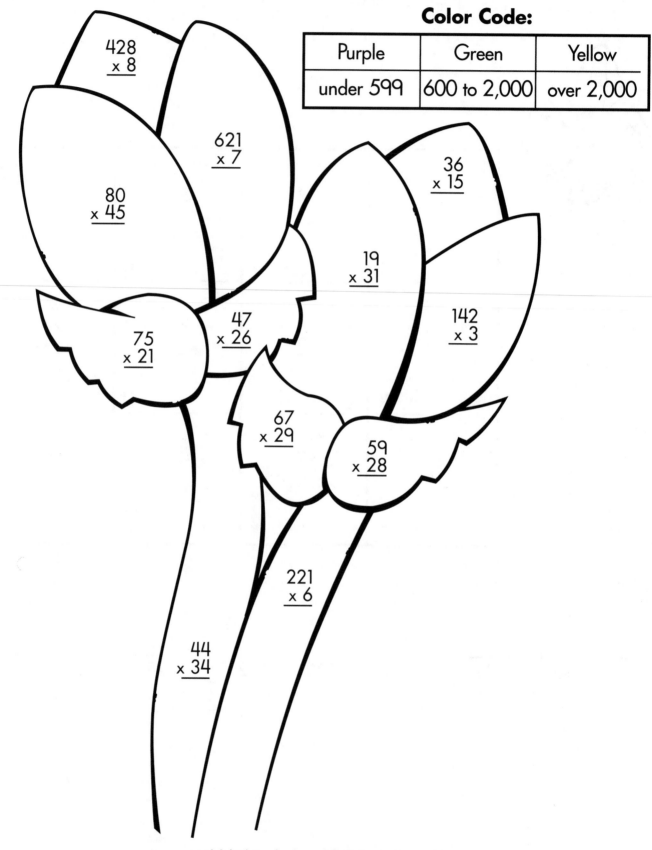

428
x 8

621
x 7

80
x 45

36
x 15

19
x 31

142
x 3

75
x 21

47
x 26

67
x 29

59
x 28

221
x 6

44
x 34

Multiplying by 1- and 2-digit numbers

Multiplying is a Blast!

Multiply.

$$335 \times 34$$

$$468 \times 23$$

$$608 \times 19$$

$$843 \times 10$$

$$879 \times 92$$

$$419 \times 41$$

$$224 \times 16$$

$$310 \times 99$$

$$479 \times 18$$

$$718 \times 39$$

$$617 \times 25$$

$$518 \times 29$$

$$244 \times 16$$

$$197 \times 31$$

$$167 \times 76$$

$$718 \times 13$$

$$517 \times 49$$

$$732 \times 50$$

$$577 \times 65$$

$$833 \times 16$$

$$619 \times 51$$

$$729 \times 23$$

$$918 \times 43$$

$$419 \times 23$$

$$245 \times 91$$

$$413 \times 43$$

$$189 \times 17$$

Multiplying 3-digit numbers by 2-digit numbers

Put the Pieces Together

$$
\begin{array}{r}
\overset{2\ \ 1\ 1}{2,432} \\
\times\ 16 \\
\hline
14592 \\
+\ 24\,320 \\
\hline
\mathbf{38,912}
\end{array}
$$
← Add a zero because you're multiplying in the tens place.

Multiply.

4,617 × 19	6,704 × 25	2,280 × 12	8,689 × 56	6,351 × 41
6,281 × 29	1,579 × 27	5,724 × 34	1,926 × 37	7,813 × 83
5,117 × 46	3,410 × 57	1,039 × 76	4,759 × 75	8,348 × 44
6,912 × 18	5,458 × 47	3,332 × 24	5,685 × 93	7,315 × 64
8,005 × 34	4,798 × 72	6,201 × 49	3,029 × 99	5,652 × 26

Multiplying 4-digit numbers by 2-digit numbers

Multiply Three by Three

```
   263
 x 146
  1578
 10520  ← Add a zero because you're multiplying in the tens place.
+26300  ← Add two zeroes because you're multiplying in the hundreds place.
 38398
```

Three Times the Fun!

Multiply.

126 x 158	325 x 122	401 x 241	836 x 425	406 x 134
227 x 114	531 x 289	200 x 146	637 x 741	342 x 300
476 x 220	512 x 478	339 x 157	741 x 335	874 x 209
986 x 608	678 x 385	425 x 227	507 x 524	805 x 775

Make a Match

Divide. Then draw a line to the matching quotients.

4)4,123   67r3

3)914   58r6

7)7,656   304r2

9)606   1,030r3

8)470   1,093r5

6)321   128r2

5)642   748r1

7)426   53r3

7)3,478   60r6

2)1,497   496r6

14

Keep it Up, Up, Up!

Divide.

```
    52 r8
16 )840
  -80↓
    40
   -32
     8
```

12)670

12)905

Now you are dividing with remainders.

15)984

36)795

36)592

45)976

40)862

23)860

21)780

14)294

37)783

43)917

19)276

16)984

26)848

14)881

18)454

21)883

20)495

22)871

13)633

20)877

38)982

18)537

Crack the Code

Divide. Then use the code to solve the riddle.

Letter Code:

2 r38 = −	12 = o	21 = k
3 r30 = q	15 = t	23 = e
5 r4 = s	16 = h	27 = p
6 = !	19 = r	28 r6 = m
7 = a	20 r7 = l	29 r7 = i

At which store did the dog lose its tail?

At the

44⟌4,123	36⟌828	54⟌146	29⟌435	21⟌147	18⟌529	15⟌307
r						

(handwritten: 19 above 44⟌4,123)

42⟌214	16⟌256	53⟌636	34⟌918	40⟌240

Dividing 3-digit dividends by 2-digit divisors

Division Skills are Blooming!

Divide.

Watch out for remainders!

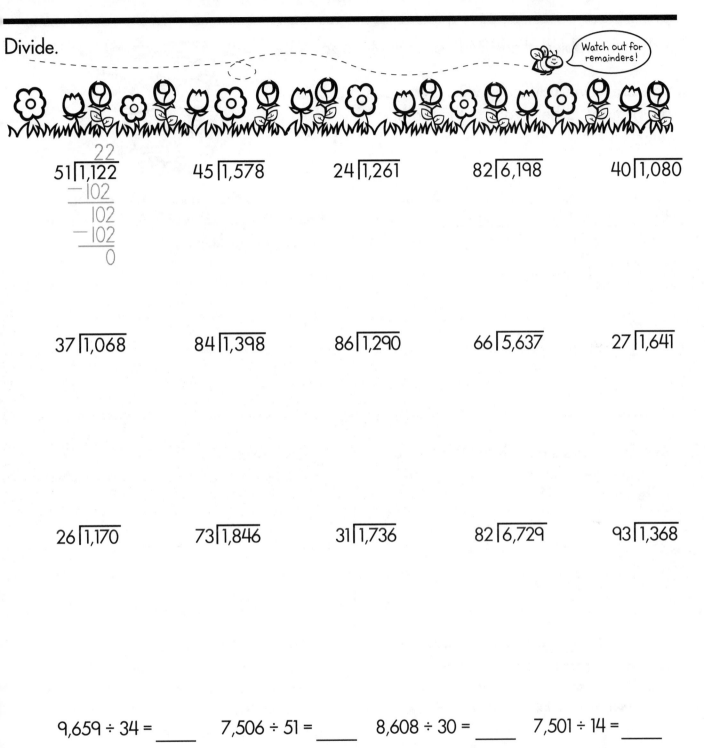

$$51\overline{)1{,}122}$$

```
    22
51)1,122
  -102
   102
  -102
     0
```

$$45\overline{)1{,}578}$$

$$24\overline{)1{,}261}$$

$$82\overline{)6{,}198}$$

$$40\overline{)1{,}080}$$

$$37\overline{)1{,}068}$$

$$84\overline{)1{,}398}$$

$$86\overline{)1{,}290}$$

$$66\overline{)5{,}637}$$

$$27\overline{)1{,}641}$$

$$26\overline{)1{,}170}$$

$$73\overline{)1{,}846}$$

$$31\overline{)1{,}736}$$

$$82\overline{)6{,}729}$$

$$93\overline{)1{,}368}$$

$9{,}659 \div 34 = \underline{\hspace{1cm}}$ $7{,}506 \div 51 = \underline{\hspace{1cm}}$ $8{,}608 \div 30 = \underline{\hspace{1cm}}$ $7{,}501 \div 14 = \underline{\hspace{1cm}}$

The Grocery Hang Out

Read each problem then divide or multiply to solve it.

If you are having difficulty with any of these problems, draw pictures to help you do the math.

1. Johnny needs to buy chicken for a Mexican fiesta. He can buy seven packages of chicken for $26.25. How much does each package of chicken cost?

2. Katie needs cucumbers for a salad. She bought five cucumbers for $2.55. What is the cost per cucumber?

3. A grocery store clerk stacked cereal boxes in rows of 40 across on a shelf. He made six rows of boxes. How many boxes of cereal were stacked in all?

4. Mrs. Smith buys three cases of juice boxes for her fifth grade class. Each case costs $2.50 and contains 12 juice boxes. How much does Mrs. Smith pay for all the juice?

5. Julie and her friends go to the store. Julie has $40.00 that she wants to share equally with her seven friends. How much money does each girl get?

6. Abbey and her friends decide to buy five bags of candy. There were 45 pieces of candy in each bag. What is the total number of pieces that Abbey and her friends shared?

Solving word problems using multiplication and division

Mean, Median, Mode

Test Scores
100 87 70 95 88 90 60 100

Mean: 86
Median: 89
Mode: 100

Mean is another word for average.
Median is the middle number in a group of numbers that have been ordered.
60 70 87 88 (**89 is between 88 and 90**) 90 95 100 100
Mode is the number that appears the most often.

Find the mean, median, and mode for each.

Basketball Points
6   22   12   36   19

Mean:_____
Median:_____
Mode:_____

Golf Scores
93   70   90   90   68   75

Mean:_____
Median:_____
Mode:_____

Data	mean	median	mode
10, 17, 10, 14, 19			
18, 19, 64, 19, 32, 60, 61			
11, 38, 13, 38, 40			
12, 15, 11, 15, 13, 10, 15			
87, 81, 95, 79, 83, 79			
96, 62, 97, 100, 96, 87, 85			

What am I?

A **prime** number is only divisible by the number 1 and itself.
A **composite** number is divisible by more than 1 and itself.

The number 2 has only two factors, which are 1 and 2 (itself).
It is only divisible by these factors. Therefore, 2 is a prime number.

The number 4 has 1, 2, and 4 as factors so it is divisible by
more than 1 and itself. Therefore, 4 is a composite number.

Look at each number. Write **P** if it is a prime number or **C** if it is a composite number.
Circle the even numbers.

9	22	5	17	51	42	73	13
C	—	—	—	—	—	—	—

49	14	19	29	32	81	25	39
—	—	—	—	—	—	—	—

64	78	91	54	94	45	27	83
—	—	—	—	—	—	—	—

12	89	68	103	34	47	109	122
—	—	—	—	—	—	—	—

74	33	58	44	87	94	40	52
—	—	—	—	—	—	—	—

61	115	107	67	51	43	58	105
—	—	—	—	—	—	—	—

93	83	72	38	25	15	88	34
—	—	—	—	—	—	—	—

Identifying prime and composite numbers

Action Fractions

Find the sum or difference in its simplest form.

$\frac{8}{18} + \frac{2}{18} = \frac{10}{18} = \frac{5}{9}$ $\qquad$ $\frac{9}{24} - \frac{5}{24} =$

$\frac{7}{13} - \frac{5}{13} =$ $\qquad$ $\frac{7}{18} - \frac{2}{18} =$

$\frac{1}{8} + \frac{7}{8} =$ $\qquad$ $\frac{10}{32} + \frac{12}{32} =$

$\frac{10}{20} - \frac{5}{20} =$ $\qquad$ $\frac{22}{30} + \frac{3}{30} =$

$\frac{8}{32} + \frac{14}{32} =$ $\qquad$ $\frac{9}{18} + \frac{9}{18} =$

$\frac{14}{26} + \frac{12}{26} =$ $\qquad$ $\frac{13}{22} + \frac{9}{22} =$

$\frac{24}{40} - \frac{8}{40} =$ $\qquad$ $\frac{9}{30} - \frac{3}{30} =$

$\frac{14}{28} - \frac{7}{28} =$ $\qquad$ $\frac{24}{42} - \frac{10}{42} =$

Action!

Adding Fractions with Common Denominators

Fractions that have a common denominator are called like fractions.

Solve the problems.

Carla walked $\frac{7}{8}$ of a mile on Monday, $\frac{6}{8}$ mile on Tuesday, and $\frac{4}{8}$ of a mile on Wednesday. How far did Carla walk in all?	Joey swam the butterfly stroke for $\frac{7}{10}$ of a mile and freestyle for $\frac{8}{10}$ of a mile. How far did Joey swim in all?
On Tuesday, Olivia and her friend pedaled $2\frac{3}{4}$ of a mile. Wednesday, they increased their mileage by $1\frac{2}{4}$ of a mile. How far did they pedal over both days?	This week Jenny bought fabric for two dresses. One dress required $3\frac{5}{8}$ yards of fabric and the other called for $4\frac{5}{8}$ yards. How much fabric did Jenny buy in all? **Challenge:** How many feet does this convert to? How many inches?

What Do We Have in Common?

To add or subtract fractions with different denominators, find the least common multiple (LCM) of each denominator, which then becomes the lowest common denominator (LCD).
To add $\frac{2}{3} + \frac{1}{4}$, find the LCM of both denominators.

Multiples of 3: 3, 6, 9, **12**, 15   12 is the LCM, so it becomes the LCD in the equation.
Multiples of 4: 4, 8, **12**, 16

Divide the LCD by each old denominator, then multiply the old numerators by the quotient.

LCD		Old Denominator		Old Quotient		Old Numerator		New Numerator		
12	÷	3	=	4	x	2	=	8	$\frac{2}{3}$ becomes	$\frac{8}{12}$
12	÷	4	=	3	x	1	=	3	$\frac{1}{4}$ becomes	$\frac{3}{12}$

Find the LCM/LCD for each pair fractions and convert to like fractions.

$\frac{2}{4}$ $\frac{6}{6}$	$\frac{2}{5}$ $\frac{4}{10}$
$\frac{7}{8}$ $\frac{3}{4}$	$\frac{2}{3}$ $\frac{3}{4}$
$\frac{4}{7}$ $\frac{2}{3}$	$\frac{5}{6}$ $\frac{7}{8}$
$\frac{7}{9}$ $\frac{1}{6}$	$\frac{3}{7}$ $\frac{1}{2}$
$\frac{3}{6}$ $\frac{1}{4}$	$\frac{5}{6}$ $\frac{4}{8}$
$\frac{2}{8}$ $\frac{2}{6}$	$\frac{1}{3}$ $\frac{3}{6}$
$\frac{1}{2}$ $\frac{3}{5}$	$\frac{3}{5}$ $\frac{1}{3}$
$\frac{3}{4}$ $\frac{1}{2}$	$\frac{1}{9}$ $\frac{1}{5}$

Simple Comparisons

Convert to like fractions, then compare using the symbols <, =, or >. Circle each fraction whose value is greater than $\frac{1}{2}$.

Comparing fractions is easier when they are like.

$\frac{5}{8}$ __ $\frac{4}{12}$ $\left(\frac{15}{24}\right) > \frac{8}{24}$ $\frac{5}{6}$ __ $\frac{3}{9}$

$\frac{4}{12}$ __ $\frac{3}{6}$ $\frac{3}{7}$ __ $\frac{2}{3}$

$\frac{7}{10}$ __ $\frac{3}{4}$ $\frac{9}{12}$ __ $\frac{3}{8}$

$\frac{3}{5}$ __ $\frac{2}{4}$ $\frac{3}{4}$ __ $\frac{2}{3}$ $\frac{1}{3}$ __ $\frac{5}{6}$

$\frac{10}{12}$ __ $\frac{2}{3}$ $\frac{1}{4}$ __ $\frac{3}{7}$ $\frac{2}{6}$ __ $\frac{2}{3}$

$\frac{4}{9}$ __ $\frac{1}{2}$ $\frac{8}{15}$ __ $\frac{5}{6}$ $\frac{7}{9}$ __ $\frac{2}{3}$

$\frac{7}{8}$ __ $\frac{2}{3}$ $\frac{7}{8}$ __ $\frac{1}{2}$ $\frac{5}{8}$ __ $\frac{2}{4}$

$\frac{3}{5}$ __ $\frac{1}{2}$ $\frac{4}{9}$ __ $\frac{1}{3}$ $\frac{4}{8}$ __ $\frac{3}{6}$

Convert to like fractions, then put them in order from **least to greatest**.

$\frac{1}{9}, \frac{1}{12}, \frac{1}{6}$ _____ $\frac{3}{16}, \frac{1}{8}, \frac{3}{4}$ _____

$\frac{6}{12}, \frac{5}{6}, \frac{2}{9}$ _____ $\frac{4}{5}, \frac{2}{10}, \frac{9}{15}$ _____

$\frac{7}{12}, \frac{5}{6}, \frac{2}{4}$ _____ $\frac{2}{3}, \frac{1}{5}, \frac{8}{10}$ _____

Finding the lowest common denominator; ordering fractions

Make Them Like!

Add the fractions. Then simplify the sum if you can.

$\frac{2}{5} + \frac{1}{3} = \frac{6}{15} + \frac{5}{15} = \frac{11}{15}$	$\frac{4}{7} + \frac{2}{4} =$	$\frac{7}{9} + \frac{1}{2} =$	$\frac{1}{3} + \frac{2}{6} =$
$\frac{5}{6} + \frac{2}{5} =$	$\frac{2}{3} + \frac{1}{4} =$	$\frac{4}{6} + \frac{5}{8} =$	$\frac{4}{7} + \frac{1}{3} =$
$\frac{8}{10} + \frac{4}{5} =$	$\frac{2}{3} + \frac{5}{6} =$	$\frac{7}{9} + \frac{1}{3} =$	$\frac{8}{10} + \frac{2}{5} =$
$\frac{4}{12} + \frac{3}{8} =$	$\frac{4}{5} + \frac{1}{3} =$	$\frac{8}{15} + \frac{5}{6} =$	$\frac{4}{7} + \frac{2}{3} =$
$\frac{9}{11} + \frac{1}{2} =$	$\frac{7}{15} + \frac{4}{6} =$	$\frac{1}{5} + \frac{5}{6} =$	$\frac{5}{12} + \frac{3}{4} =$
$\frac{4}{5} + \frac{7}{8} =$	$\frac{9}{15} + \frac{4}{9} =$	$\frac{7}{18} + \frac{3}{4} =$	$\frac{2}{9} + \frac{1}{2} =$

Adding fractions with unlike denominators; simplifying fractions

Simple Subtraction with Fractions

Don't forget to find the LCD!

It's simple!

Subtract the fractions.
Then simplify the difference if you can.

$\frac{7}{8} - \frac{1}{2} = \frac{7}{8} - \frac{4}{8} = \frac{3}{8}$	$\frac{6}{7} - \frac{2}{3} =$	$\frac{7}{9} - \frac{1}{4} =$	$\frac{6}{8} - \frac{2}{4} =$
$\frac{11}{15} - \frac{3}{5} =$	$\frac{5}{6} - \frac{2}{8} =$	$\frac{5}{7} - \frac{2}{4} =$	$\frac{11}{15} - \frac{2}{5} =$
$\frac{13}{15} - \frac{4}{6} =$	$\frac{7}{12} - \frac{4}{9} =$	$\frac{9}{10} - \frac{7}{15} =$	$\frac{10}{25} - \frac{5}{20} =$
$\frac{5}{6} - \frac{1}{3} =$	$\frac{4}{5} - \frac{1}{3} =$	$\frac{8}{11} - \frac{1}{4} =$	$\frac{4}{8} - \frac{2}{16} =$
$\frac{3}{9} - \frac{2}{6} =$	$\frac{2}{3} - \frac{2}{7} =$	$\frac{8}{15} - \frac{2}{5} =$	$\frac{3}{9} - \frac{1}{3} =$
$\frac{6}{8} - \frac{2}{3} =$	$\frac{9}{18} - \frac{2}{3} =$	$\frac{13}{14} - \frac{3}{7} =$	$\frac{7}{9} - \frac{5}{36} =$

Subtracting fractions with unlike denominators; simplifying fractions

Picking Up The Pace!

To add mixed numerals, find the lowest common denominator.

$$5\frac{4}{7} + 3\frac{1}{3} = 5\frac{12}{21} + 3\frac{7}{21} = 8\frac{19}{21}$$

To subtract mixed numerals, find the lowest common denominator, too. Sometimes, you will need to regroup.

$$5\frac{3}{4} - 2\frac{5}{6} = 5\frac{9}{12} - 2\frac{10}{12}$$

Regroup 1 whole, or 12 parts, from the whole number 5.
Add the 12 parts to your numerator, 9.

$$5\frac{9}{12} = 4\frac{21}{12}$$

$$4\frac{21}{12} - 2\frac{10}{12} = 2\frac{11}{12}$$

Solve the problems.

$4\frac{2}{3} + 3\frac{1}{4} =$ $6\frac{4}{7} + 8\frac{1}{3} =$ $7\frac{3}{8} + 2\frac{8}{12} =$

$6\frac{2}{3} + 3\frac{3}{4} =$ $9\frac{4}{5} - 7\frac{2}{3} =$ $12\frac{4}{9} - 4\frac{5}{6} =$

$14\frac{4}{6} + 3\frac{5}{8} =$ $7\frac{4}{12} + 4\frac{3}{6} =$ $5\frac{4}{5} + 2\frac{1}{3} =$

$7\frac{4}{5} - 4\frac{1}{4} =$ $10\frac{4}{8} - 4\frac{5}{6} =$ $12\frac{4}{8} - 3\frac{4}{5} =$

$10\frac{1}{2} + 5\frac{2}{8} =$ $9\frac{4}{16} + 3\frac{5}{8} =$ $2\frac{7}{9} + 4\frac{1}{2} =$

Adding and subtracting mixed numerals

Everything is Multiplying!

$\frac{3}{8} \times \frac{4}{5} = \frac{12}{40}$ ⟵ Multiply the numerators.
⟵ Multiply the denominator.

Then simplify the answer if you can.

$\frac{12}{40} = \frac{3}{10}$

It's multiplying!

Multiply the fractions. Then simplify the product if you can.

$\frac{5}{6} \times \frac{7}{8} =$	$\frac{4}{5} \times \frac{6}{7} =$	$\frac{7}{9} \times \frac{4}{5} =$	$\frac{8}{9} \times \frac{2}{3} =$
$\frac{4}{8} \times \frac{3}{5} =$	$\frac{9}{10} \times \frac{2}{7} =$	$\frac{5}{7} \times \frac{9}{11} =$	$\frac{6}{9} \times \frac{2}{6} =$
$\frac{4}{6} \times \frac{7}{9} =$	$\frac{3}{6} \times \frac{7}{10} =$	$\frac{4}{7} \times \frac{2}{3} =$	$\frac{5}{8} \times \frac{7}{9} =$
$\frac{6}{12} \times \frac{1}{2} =$	$\frac{3}{4} \times \frac{7}{8} =$	$\frac{3}{4} \times \frac{6}{7} =$	$\frac{5}{9} \times \frac{4}{10} =$
$\frac{1}{11} \times \frac{4}{5} =$	$\frac{8}{10} \times \frac{4}{6} =$	$\frac{3}{9} \times \frac{2}{3} =$	$\frac{4}{6} \times \frac{5}{4} =$
$\frac{4}{6} \times \frac{3}{12} =$	$\frac{3}{9} \times \frac{7}{8} =$	$\frac{1}{4} \times \frac{3}{6} =$	$\frac{8}{9} \times \frac{1}{3} =$

Multiplying by Fractions

An easy recipe for multiplying whole numbers by fractions.

$$6 \times \frac{3}{4} = 6 \times \frac{3}{3} = \frac{6}{1} \times \frac{3}{4} = \frac{18}{4} = 4\frac{2}{4} = 4\frac{1}{2}$$

Take the whole number 6.
Place a 1 under it to make it a fraction.
Then multiply the fractions.
For a well-done product, remember to make
the fraction proper and simplify!

Multiply.

$5 \times \frac{3}{4}$ = _____

$8 \times \frac{1}{3}$ = _____

$7 \times \frac{4}{9}$ = _____

$9 \times \frac{3}{5}$ = _____

$4 \times \frac{1}{2}$ = _____

$6 \times \frac{2}{5}$ = _____

$4 \times \frac{2}{9}$ = _____

$2 \times \frac{4}{12}$ = _____

$5 \times \frac{4}{16}$ = _____

$3 \times \frac{5}{7}$ = _____

$7 \times \frac{4}{15}$ = _____

$8 \times \frac{4}{5}$ = _____

$10 \times \frac{3}{15}$ = _____

$12 \times \frac{3}{6}$ = _____

$7 \times \frac{4}{7}$ = _____

What is $\frac{1}{9}$ of 45? _____

What is $\frac{1}{4}$ of 16? _____

What is $\frac{1}{4}$ of 20? _____

What is $\frac{3}{8}$ of 4? _____

What is $\frac{2}{3}$ of 8? _____

What is $\frac{1}{8}$ of 26? _____

Flipping over Division

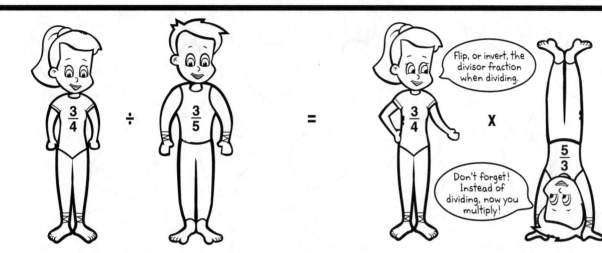

Divide the fractions. Show your work.

$\frac{4}{6} \div \frac{1}{3} = \frac{4}{6} \times \frac{3}{1} = \frac{12}{6} = 2$	$\frac{5}{7} \div \frac{2}{3} =$
$\frac{6}{8} \div \frac{4}{5} =$	$\frac{5}{9} \div \frac{2}{7} =$
$\frac{5}{8} \div \frac{2}{6} =$	$\frac{3}{6} \div \frac{2}{7} =$
$\frac{8}{10} \div \frac{3}{6} =$	$\frac{3}{5} \div \frac{1}{2} =$
$\frac{3}{4} \div \frac{1}{5} =$	$\frac{4}{8} \div \frac{1}{3} =$
$\frac{1}{3} \div \frac{1}{4} =$	$\frac{1}{4} \div \frac{4}{5} =$
$\frac{4}{9} \div \frac{2}{6} =$	$\frac{7}{9} \div \frac{3}{6} =$
$\frac{3}{5} \div \frac{4}{7} =$	$\frac{2}{4} \div \frac{1}{3} =$
$\frac{9}{10} \div \frac{3}{4} =$	
$\frac{6}{8} \div \frac{7}{9} =$	
$\frac{3}{5} \div \frac{4}{8} =$	
$\frac{6}{9} \div \frac{1}{4} =$	

Fruity Fractions

Write the answers.

1. How many pieces of fruit are in the set?_____

2. What fraction of the set do the bananas represent?_____

3. What fraction of the set do the apples represent?_____

4. What fraction of the set do the pineapples represent?_____

5. What fraction of the set do the pears represent?_____

6. What fraction of the set do the oranges represent?_____

7. Which fruit makes up $\frac{1}{3}$ of the set? _____

8. Which fruit makes up $\frac{1}{6}$ of the set? _____

9. What two combinations of fruit each make up one half of the set?

_____ and _____

Solving fraction word problems

Dealing with Decimals

Use the place value chart at the right to help you name decimal values.

Let's get this straight.

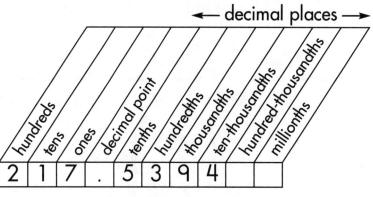

The number **217.5394** is read as "two hundred seventeen and five thousand, three hundred ninety-four ten-thousandths."

Tip: Do not write a comma between place values for the numerals after the decimal point.

Write the place value of the last digit in each number.

6.7328 _____   4.395 _____

43.39 _____   2.43893 _____

0.514 _____   13.81573 _____

Write each numeral in written form. Don't forget to use "and."

23.7 _____

2.49 _____

1.297 _____

1.0005 _____

21.006 _____

3.00009 _____

0.984 _____

Write each number in standard form.

fourteen and nine tenths _____   nine and ten thousandths_____

six hundred fifty and seven thousandths_____   ninety-one and four thousandths _____

eighty-four and seven hundredths_____   one and nine millionths_____

Understanding decimals; identifying decimal place values

Decimal Double Take

The same amount can be written as a fraction or a decimal.

.6 is also $\frac{6}{10}$

Write the correct letters to match the fractions and decimals.

$\frac{34}{100}$	D	**A)** .60	$\frac{83}{100}$ ___	**N)** $\frac{61}{100}$	
.57 ___		**B)** $\frac{2}{10}$	$\frac{6}{10}$ ___	**O)** $\frac{91}{100}$	
$\frac{42}{100}$ ___		**C)** $\frac{54}{100}$	$\frac{9}{10}$ ___	**P)** .83	
$\frac{60}{100}$ ___		**D)** .34	.91 ___	**Q)** .6	
.79 ___		**E)** $\frac{41}{100}$	.64 ___	**R)** .1	
.341 ___		**F)** .98	$\frac{512}{1000}$ ___	**S)** $\frac{57}{100}$	
.41 ___		**G)** $\frac{79}{100}$	$\frac{1}{10}$ ___	**T)** .33	
$\frac{27}{100}$ ___		**H)** .29	$\frac{114}{100}$ ___	**U)** .19	
$\frac{98}{100}$ ___		**I)** .42	$\frac{33}{100}$ ___	**V)** .114	
$\frac{29}{100}$ ___		**J)** $\frac{341}{1000}$	.57 ___	**W)** .08	
.2 ___		**K)** $\frac{57}{100}$	$\frac{19}{100}$ ___	**X)** $\frac{64}{100}$	
.7 ___		**L)** .27	$\frac{8}{100}$ ___	**Y)** .9	
.54 ___		**M)** $\frac{7}{10}$	.61 ___	**Z)** .512	

Recognizing equivalent decimals and fractions

Get the Point?

To change a percent to a decimal, move the decimal point two places to the left and drop the percent sign.

44% = .44

Change each percent to a decimal.

90% = _____   48% = _____   28% = _____   29% = _____   3% = _____

12% = _____   64% = _____   79% = _____   24% = _____   65% = _____

5% = _____   56% = _____   94% = _____   20% = _____   27% = _____

17% = _____   19% = _____   82% = _____   3% = _____   72% = _____

26% = _____   10% = _____   78% = _____   99% = _____   41% = _____

9% = _____   4% = _____   14% = _____   36% = _____   6% = _____

Complete the table.

Fractions	Decimals	Percents
$\frac{1}{2}$	0.5	_____
$\frac{1}{5}$	_____	20%
_____	0.625	62.5%
$\frac{1}{10}$	_____	_____
_____	0.69	69%

Rule of Thumb

Add.

```
   0.07          1.4          2.517
   2.4          23.07        34.433
+ 13.444        + 5.19      + 12.007
 15.914
```

When adding or
subtracting decimals,
always line up the
decimal points!

```
    .008          .017         2.45
  47.158          .24         0.517
 + 2.009        + 23.01      + 18.56
```

```
  83.168      514.7890      613.004       7.009       29.0004      9.5168
+ 14.009     + 78.0045     + 528.109    + 23.870     + 7.519     + 14.815
```

```
   1.807        51.88        0.0517        .0012       65.004       79.416
  23.005         0.93       16.0009      41.0809       14.013        0.008
    .235         5.09        5.0018       1.7004        1.08          3.5
 + 2.069        + 0.78       + 7.45     + 34.0098     + 23.005     + 14.98
```

Line up the decimals and solve. (Hint: Write the problems vertically!)

5.8001 + 41.9 =_____   0.915 + 2.0008 =_____   0.3 + .00078 =_____

0.54 + 8.0040 =_____   4.5 + 12.7088 =_____   3.4 + 0.0012 =_____

Adding decimals

Falling Amounts

Subtract.

No matter how they fall, line up the decimal points.

```
      51
  14.363        5.708         .407
 - 0.324       - 1.416      - 0.324
  14.039
```

```
  32.426       12.0076      51.709
 -14.018      - 0.4581    - 23.416
```

```
  51.006       0.8377       0.0138       6.527        9           0.96
 - 4.86       - 0.0451     - 0.0060     - 5.139     - 3.36       - 0.19
```

```
   8          7.00149      5.1870      12.0041      11           0.869
 - 1.98       - 2.46      - 0.408      - 4.698     - 3.149      - 0.476
```

Line up the decimals and solve. (Hint: Write the problems vertically!)

6.03 – .49 = _____   23.7 – 4.092 = _____   14.907 – 0.989 = _____

3.410 – .891= _____   12 – 0.0189 = _____   7.410 – 0.59 = _____

Little Makes BIG!

Prime factorization is writing a composite number as a product of prime factors.

To find the prime factorization of 24, only use prime numbers as factors to equal 24.

Look! These numbers are prime!

2 x 2 x 2 x 3

4 x 2 x 3

8 x 3 = 24

Draw a line to match the number to its factorization.
(Hint: The answers must be entirely in prime numbers.)

72	• 2 x 5 x 5 • 2 x 36 • 2 x 2 x 2 x 3 x 3	77	• 3 x 3 x 3 x 3 x 2 • 2 x 3 x 7 • 7 x 11
81	• 3 x 3 x 3 x 3 • 3 x 3 x 3 x 7 • 3 x 3 x 5	48	• 2 x 2 x 2 x 2 x 36 • 3 x 2 x 2 x 2 x 2 • 7 x 2 x 2
36	• 3 x 3 x 3 x 9 • 2 x 2 x 5 • 2 x 2 x 3 x 3	45	• 3 x 3 x 5 • 2 x 2 x 2 x 3 • 3 x 5

Write the prime factorization for the following numbers.

28 _____   72 _____

16 _____   144 _____

21 _____   56 _____

18 _____   64 _____

27 _____   42 _____

Find the product.

3 x 5 x 5 x 11 = _____   2 x 3 x 3 = _____   2 x 2 x 2 x 3 x 3 = _____

2 x 2 x 3 x 3 x 5 = _____   3 x 7 x 7 = _____   2 x 2 x 5 = _____

Understanding prime factorization

Keeping Track of Those Decimals!

```
  83.4        1    There is 1 digit to the right of the decimal point.
 x .12      + 2    There are 2 digits to the right of the decimal point
 1668         3    There are 3 digits to the right of the decimal point.
+ 834↓
10.008             There is a total of 3 digits to the right of the decimal point in the product.
```

Multiply.

14.6 x 0.7	18.35 x 1.6	7.89 x 1.40	91.04 x 9.00	0.075 x 1.07	0.516 x 0.14
0.003 x .51	0.415 x .71	0.12 x .56	1.006 x 0.98	0.32 x 0.517	10.147 x .076
0.256 x .145	0.00124 x .432	0.4196 x .981	0.0681 x .391	0.616 x .51	1.519 x .35
12.5 x 5.9	9.710 x .02	3.0058 x .539	15.98 x 2.09	1.209 x 8.159	1.097 x 0.07

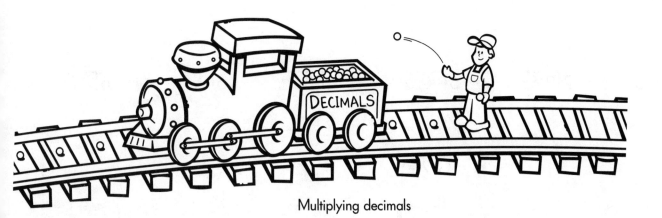

Multiplying decimals

Razzle Dazzle Decimals

Divide.

$$\begin{array}{r} 1.3 \\ 3\overline{)3.9} \\ -3 \\ \hline 9 \\ -9 \\ \hline \end{array}$$

$5\overline{)5.4}$ $3\overline{)7.29}$ $5\overline{)37.5}$ $8\overline{)88.8}$ $7\overline{)6.37}$

$9\overline{)40.5}$ $3\overline{)2.25}$ $7\overline{)6.51}$ $2\overline{)9.22}$ $5\overline{)102.7}$ $2\overline{)4.42}$

$3\overline{)4.41}$ $2\overline{)9.87}$ $2\overline{)7.9}$ $3\overline{)9.6}$ $6\overline{)24.0}$ $9\overline{)80.1}$

$8\overline{)65.2}$ $4\overline{)25.6}$ $4\overline{)2.96}$ $8\overline{)36.2}$ $4\overline{)1.6}$ $7\overline{)8.05}$

$2\overline{)66.3}$ $2\overline{)9.68}$ $5\overline{)40.5}$ $8\overline{)48.2}$ $5\overline{)2.5}$ $6\overline{)7.2}$

Dividing with decimals

Exploring Decimal Division

$1.6\overline{)9.6}$

$1.6 \times 10 = 16.0$
$9.6 \times 10 = 96.0$

First, convert the divisor into a whole number by multiplying the divisor and dividend by 10.

─── **decimal point**

$$\begin{array}{r} 6.0 \\ 16\overline{)96.0} \\ \underline{96} \end{array}$$

Next, place the decimal point in the quotient and divide as with whole numbers.

Divide.

$3.2\overline{)2.24}$ $2.8\overline{)4.48}$ $8.2\overline{)229.6}$ $0.05\overline{)42.5}$ $1.1\overline{)5.5}$ $0.18\overline{)6.3}$

$2.7\overline{)22.41}$ $0.13\overline{)0.026}$ $0.6\overline{)806.4}$ $1.2\overline{)0.876}$ $0.02\overline{).158}$ $0.16\overline{)0.624}$

$4.9\overline{)2.499}$ $.91\overline{)6.734}$ $8.7\overline{)53.244}$ $0.04\overline{).2528}$ $0.3\overline{)9}$ $0.8\overline{)0.4168}$

$0.5\overline{)3.125}$ $3.3\overline{)13.86}$ $0.7\overline{)5.32}$ $0.3\overline{)0.192}$ $.005\overline{)6.3}$ $6.3\overline{)9.765}$

Dividing with decimals in the dividend and divisor

Expanding With Exponents

A **power** is the product of multiplying a number by itself. It is represented as a **base number** and an **exponent**.
The **base number** indicates what number is being multiplied, and the **exponent** indicates how many times the base number is to be multiplied.

$$10^{\overset{\text{exponent}}{5}} = \underbrace{10 \times 10 \times 10 \times 10 \times 10}_{\text{factors}} = 100{,}000$$

base number

Write the factors, then find the value.

$5^2 =$ $7^3 =$ $9^3 =$ $3^4 =$ $2^3 =$
$5 \times 5 = 25$

$10^6 =$ $10^4 =$ $5^4 =$ $6^6 =$ $3^5 =$

Write the value.

$7^2 = 49$ $9^5 =$ $4^4 =$ $2^5 =$ $1^9 =$

$8^1 =$ $3^2 =$ $2^7 =$ $3^4 =$ $8^2 =$

Write the value using exponents.

$5 \times 5 \times 5 \times 5 \times 5 =$ $10 \times 10 \times 10 \times 10 \times 10 =$ $6 \times 6 \times 6 \times 6 =$ $2 \times 2 =$

$4 \times 4 \times 4 \times 4 =$ $7 \times 7 \times 7 =$ $2 \times 2 \times 2 \times 2 \times 2 =$ $3 \times 3 \times 3 =$

$10 \times 10 \times 10 =$ $5 \times 5 =$ $8 \times 8 \times 8 =$ $10 \times 10 =$

Fill in the missing numbers.

Product	Number to Given Power	Standard Notation
$8 \times 8 \times 8$	8^3	512
5×5		
	12^3	
$2 \times 2 \times 2 \times 2 \times 2$		

Slurping Down Cubes and Squares

The **square** of a number is the number times itself.

$$5^2 = 5 \times 5 = 25$$

The **cube** of a number is the number multiplied twice by itself.

$$5^3 = 5 \times 5 \times 5 = 125$$

Write the square or cube of each number.

$4^2 =$ ___4 x 4 = 16___ $9^2 =$ _____ $3^3 =$ _____

$6^3 =$ _____ $7^2 =$ _____ $15^3 =$ _____

$10^3 =$ _____ $5^3 =$ _____ $14^2 =$ _____

$20^2 =$ _____ $24^3 =$ _____ $19^3 =$ _____

$8^3 =$ _____ $13^2 =$ _____ $48^2 =$ _____

$17^2 =$ _____ $25^3 =$ _____ $37^2 =$ _____

Write the square root.

$36 =$ ___6^2___ $64 =$ _____ $81 =$ _____ $25 =$ _____ $324 =$ _____ $529 =$ _____

$100 =$ _____ $49 =$ _____ $4 =$ _____ $16 =$ _____ $121 =$ _____ $1{,}600 =$ _____

$400 =$ _____ $225 =$ _____ $625 =$ _____ $144 =$ _____ $900 =$ _____ $2{,}500 =$ _____

Write the cube root.

$125 =$ ___5^3___ $1{,}000 =$ ____ $64 =$ _____ $27 =$ _____ $8 =$ _____ $216 =$ _____

$512 =$ _____ $1{,}728 =$ ____ $2{,}744 =$ ____ $343 =$ _____ $8{,}000 =$ ____ $6{,}859 =$ _____

Powerful Probability

Answer each question using a statement and a fraction.

What's the Likelihood?

1. Maggie has a bag of marbles with eight purple marbles, five orange marbles, four blue, and seven green. How many marbles does Maggie have in all? 24

    (8 + 5 + 4 + 7)

    What are Maggie's chances of picking a blue marble?

    Her chances of picking a blue marble are 4 in 24.

2. Jesse is trying to draw a queen from a deck of 52 playing cards. If he already drew one card with no luck, what is the probability of him drawing a queen now?

    What is the probability of drawing a queen on the third try if a queen hasn't been drawn yet?

3. If there are nine boys and 13 girls in the gym class and a student closes his eyes to pick a person for his team, is he more likely to pick a boy or a girl?

    What are the chances of picking a boy?

    What are the chances of picking a girl?

4. Penny's large pack of gum contains five strawberry flavored pieces, three lime flavored pieces, and eight lemon flavored pieces. If Penny pulls out a piece without looking, what flavor is she most likely to get?

    What are the probabilities of each flavor being chosen?

5. A bag of colorful shelled candy contains eight orange, four green, seven yellow, three blue, six red, and seven brown pieces.

    What is the probability of drawing a green or yellow piece of candy?

    What is the probability of drawing an orange or blue piece?

    Which color candy is likely to be drawn?

6. A dart board has 14 spaces that show even numbers between 3 and 31 and ten spaces that show odd numbers from 3 to 21. What is the probability of a dart landing on a space with a prime number?

    What is the probability of a dart landing on a space with a composite number?

Terrific Tables

Complete each rate table, then answer the questions.

Mr. Petz has a chicken farm. He is able to collect 60 dozen eggs per week from his chickens.

Dozen	60									
Week	1	2	3	4	5	6	7	8	9	10

How many dozen eggs does Mr. Petz collect in a six-week period?

If there are four weeks in a month, how many dozen eggs are collected in two months?

How many dozen eggs are collected in a three-month period?

Dean is taking a trip. His car will travel 30 miles per gallon of gasoline on the highway.

Miles	30									
Gallons	1	2	3	4	5	6	7	8	9	10

How far can the car travel on eight gallons of gas?

If Dean went 270 miles, how many gallons of gas did he use?

If the tank in Dean's car is completely full of gas at 15 gallons, how far can he go on one tank of gas?

The Pampered Pet Groomers can groom up to 18 dogs in a two-day period.

Pets	18									
Days	2	4	6	8	10	12	14	16	18	20

How many dogs can be groomed in a two-week period?

If there are 30 days in this month, how many pets can be groomed in the month?

If two groomers do all the grooming, how many dogs does one groomer take care of in a ten-day period?

Mix and Match Geometry

Write the correct letters to match the geometric terms to their definitions.

Quadrilateral _____

Parallelogram _____

Point _____

Right Angle _____

Acute angle _____

Obtuse angle _____

Line _____

Decagon _____

Congruent _____

Octagon _____

Pentagon _____

Heptagon _____

Nonagon _____

Dodecagon _____

Hexagon _____

Rotation _____

Translation _____

Reflection _____

Parallel _____

Perpendicular _____

A) part of a line between two end points, an exact location

B) a polygon with four sides

C) a polygon with eight sides

D) a ten-sided polygon

E) a never-ending path in the opposite direction with no endpoints

F) a quadrilateral whose opposite sides are parallel and congruent

G) a $90°$ angle

H) an angle more than $90°$

I) an angle less than $90°$

J) having the same size and shape

K) a polygon with five sides and angles

L) lines and/or line segments that are exactly the same distance apart

M) a polygon with six sides and angles

N) two lines that intersect to form four right angles

O) a polygon with twelve sides and angles

P) a polygon with nine sides and angles

Q) sliding a figure in any direction

R) turning a figure around a point

S) a polygon with seven sides and angles

T) when a figure is flipped over a line

What's My Name?

A triangle has three names. The last name is always "triangle."

The 1st name is from the angle:
Any triangle with a 90° angle is a right triangle.
Any triangle with an angle less than 90° is an acute triangle.
Any triangle with an angle greater than 90° is an obtuse triagle.

The 2nd name is from the sides:
If all sides are equal, the triangle is equilateral.
If only two sides are equal, the triangle is isosceles.
If no sides are equal, the triangle is scalene.

What is your name?

My last name is triangle.

Write the three-word name for each triangle.

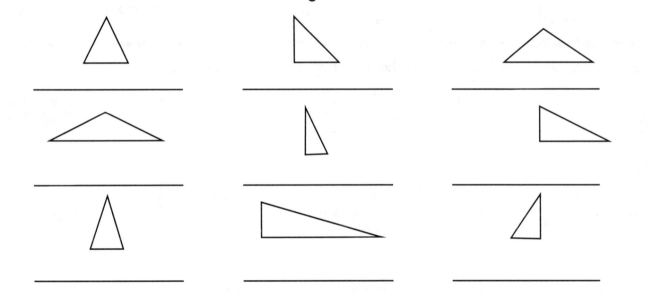

_____   _____   _____

_____   _____   _____

_____   _____   _____

Challenge yourself!
How many combinations of triangles can there be?

Find the angles listed. Write the letters that form these angles.

Example: ECF is an acute angle.

Two right angles:_____

Two obtuse angles:_____

Five acute angles:_____

Understanding triangles and angles

Inch by Inch!

U.S. Customary Measurements of Length
12 inches (in.) = 1 foot (ft.)
3 feet = 1 yard (yd.)
5,280 feet = 1 mile (mi.)
1,760 yards = 1 mile

Convert each measurement.

60 in. = _____ ft.   3 yd. = _____ in.   4 mi. = _____ in.   39 ft. = _____ in.

$4\frac{1}{2}$ mi. = _____ ft. $7\frac{5}{6}$ ft. = _____ in.   9 mi. = _____ yd.   13 yd. = _____ in.

31 mi. = _____ yd.   1,272 in. = _____ ft.   1,512 in. = _____ yd.   1,628 ft. = _____ in.

Solve, then convert each answer to the simplest expression of length.

```
   10 ft.           7 ft. 8 in.          3 yd. 5 ft.          9 mi.   870 ft.          22 yd. 9 in.
+  3 ft. 11 in.   + 8 ft. 4 in.        + 7 yd. 8 ft.       + 11 mi. 4,000 ft.       + 14 yd. 4 in.
```

```
   4 yd. 2 ft.       36 ft. 9 in.        14 yd. 4 ft.        18 mi. 178 ft.          19 yd.  3 in.
-  2 yd. 1 ft.     - 18 ft. 6 in.       - 9 yd. 3 ft.       - 1 mi.  62 ft.        - 12 yd. 10 in.
```

```
   9 yd. 2 in.       3 ft. 8 in.         15 yd. 3 ft.        23 mi. 180 yd.          12 yd. 10 in.
         x 3               x 4                  x 6                    x 5                    x 7
```

Solve.

1. Mrs. Gibson's class measured the heights of its three tallest students. Emily is five-feet four-inches tall, Blaine is five-feet tall, and William is four-feet 11 inches tall. What is the combined height of these three students?

2. There are two mountains in the town of Okeene. One is three-miles 2,480-feet high, and the other is one-mile 5,170-feet high. What is the difference in the heights?

Massive Amounts of Measurement

U.S. Customary Measurements of Liquid
1 pint (pt.) = 2 cups (c.) 1 quart (qt.) = 2 pints 1 gallon (gal.) = 4 quarts

U.S. Customary Measurements of Weight
16 ounces (oz.) = 1 pound (lb.) 2,000 pounds = 1 ton (T.)

Write the correct unit of measure.

a small juice box drink 1 _____

a basketball weighs 7_____

a truck weighs 2 _____

a horse trailer weighs 1 _____

a bag of potatoes weighs 5 _____

a set of pens weighs 4 _____

a compact disc weighs 4 _____

a washing machine holds 15 _____

a mouse weighs 5 _____

a bicycle weighs 28 _____

a container of yogurt holds 1 _____

a canoe weighs 90 _____

an apple weighs 5 _____

a swimming pool holds 1,200 _____

a flashlight weighs 2 _____

clothes in the washing machine weigh 20 _____

Convert each measurement.

6 qt. = _____ c.

9 pt. = _____ c.

3 gal. = _____ c.

14 qt. = _____ c.

16 gal. = _____ pt.

23 qt. = _____ pt.

50 gal. = _____ c.

36 qt. = _____ pt.

96 oz. = _____ lb.

132 lb. = _____ oz.

18 lb. = _____ oz.

3 T. = _____ lb.

1.8 T. = _____ oz.

48 oz. = _____ lb.

1 T 16 lb. = _____ oz.

4,000 lb. = _____ T.

34 gal. = _____ pt.

4,000 gal. = _____ qt.

346 lb. = _____ oz.

561 qt. = _____ pt.

Raving about Ratios

5 boys to 7 girls   5 to 7   5:7   5/7

Write the ratios. Show each ratio three different ways.

△ △ △ △
♡ ♡ ♡ ♡
□ □ □ □
○ ○ ○ ○

△s to all shapes 4 to 16, 4:16, $\frac{4}{16}$ (or $\frac{1}{4}$)

○s to △s _____

△s to □s _____

♡s to △s _____

△ △ △ △
△ △ ○ ○
○ ○ □ □
□ □ ♡ ◇

◇s to △s _____

□s to ○s _____

♡s to ○s _____

△s to ♡s _____

☺ ☺ ☺ ☺
△ △ △ △
△ △ △ □
□ □ □ ◇

△s to ☺s _____

□s to ☺s _____

△s to □s _____

□s to ◇s _____

⬡ ⬡ ⬡ ⬡
⬠ ⬠ ⬠ ⬠
□ □ □ □
□ □ □ ○

⬡s to □s _____

□s to ⬠s _____

⬠s to ⬡s _____

○s to ⬠s _____

Write each ratio two different ways.

7 days/week _____   24 hours/day _____   3 tickets/1 ride _____   12 cookies/2 pans _____

7 boys/9 girls _____   44 students/2 teachers _____   3 dogs/6 kids _____   24 stickers/3 pages _____

Figuring ratios

Powerful Percents

Let's change the fraction $\frac{5}{8}$ to a percent.

1st: Change the fraction to a decimal.

Divide the numerator by the denominator.
Add 0's to keep from having a remainder.

```
      .625
  8 ) 5.000
     -48
      20
     -16
      40
     -40
       0
```

A percent means per hundred. So... 25% means 25 of 100.

2nd: Move the decimal point two places to the right and add the percent sign.

.62.5 %

Change each fraction to a percent. Don't forget the percent sign.

$\frac{80}{100} =$ _____ $\frac{3}{4} =$ _____ $\frac{3}{8} =$ _____ $\frac{9}{10} =$ _____ $\frac{3}{19} =$ _____

$\frac{22}{100} =$ _____ $\frac{4}{5} =$ _____ $\frac{9}{20} =$ _____ $\frac{4}{25} =$ _____ $\frac{9}{100} =$ _____

$\frac{3}{5} =$ _____ $\frac{6}{25} =$ _____ $\frac{7}{15} =$ _____ $\frac{16}{25} =$ _____ $\frac{7}{8} =$ _____

$\frac{5}{9} =$ _____ $\frac{4}{50} =$ _____ $\frac{8}{15} =$ _____ $\frac{3}{10} =$ _____ $\frac{2}{5} =$ _____

$\frac{8}{25} =$ _____ $\frac{11}{50} =$ _____ $\frac{11}{12} =$ _____ $\frac{9}{25} =$ _____ $\frac{1}{5} =$ _____

Challenge yourself!
See how many things you can list that express percents. For example, test scores come in percents.

Reasonableness Riddles

Reasonableness is after working the problem the answer makes sense.

Write the ages.

I am five years younger than Patty, who will be 46 in seven years.

My age:_____ Patty's age:_____

Syd is seven years older than Kathy, who will be 19 in eight years.

Syd's age: _____ Kathy's age: _____

Kim is 52 years younger than her grandpa, who will be 98 in 14 years.

Kim's age:_____ Grandpa's age:_____

Dale is 19 years younger than Ann, who will be 46 in 23 years.

Dale's age: _____ Ann's age: _____

The pie chart shows the way Lucy spends her monthly income of $300. Use the chart to answer the questions.

What is a reasonable estimate of the amount of money Lucy spends on groceries?_____

What is a reasonable estimate of the amount of money Lucy spends on gas?_____

About how much does she spend on entertainment each month?_____

(pie chart: savings 25%, food 15%, misc. 10%, gas 5%, entertainment 20%, clothing 25%)

The chart below shows the percentages of the fifth and sixth grade students who named their favorite flavor of ice cream.

Ice Cream Flavor	%
Chocolate	30%
Chocolate Chip	38%
Vanilla	2%
Strawberry	9%
Cookies-and-Cream	11%
Butter Pecan	10%

If there are 370 students in fifth and sixth grade, what is the reasonable number of students who like chocolate chip?

What is the reasonable number of students who like strawberry or cookies-and-cream?

Choose three flavors which make up exactly half of the total percentage.

What is a reasonable ratio of students who chose chocolate to butter pecan?

Understanding and figuring reasonableness

Multiplication Review I

Multiply.

162 x 65	215 x 84	165 x 66	932 x 73	198 x 23	462 x 65
198 x 73	1,462 x 30	2,432 x 23	1,665 x 79	3,913 x 77	174 x 36
173 x 72	1,643 x 65	345 x 44	415 x 46	654 x 73	3,346 x 94
354 x 13	982 x 70	491 x 43	2,651 x 63	1,531 x 61	9,879 x 75
6,462 x 36	5,413 x 73	5,459 x 94	879 x 83	563 x 61	163 x 39
9,963 x 43	4,563 x 61	428 x 63	539 x 43	1,569 x 96	255 x 50

Multiplication Review II

Multiply.

654 x 865	166 x 188	235 x 365	167 x 973	933 x 425	741 x 104
199 x 371	465 x 230	432 x 796	665 x 123	923 x 679	827 x 427
173 x 721	643 x 465	346 x 446	411 x 125	654 x 733	782 x 965
354 x 123	982 x 226	497 x 376	6,651 x 569	2,531 x 331	748 x 873
462 x 256	531 x 257	449 x 821	879 x 733	448 x 104	462 x 226

Reviewing multiplication

Division Review I

Divide.

6⟌240	2⟌5,436	35⟌5,257	6⟌1,224	4⟌573	6⟌513
3⟌7,564	9⟌1,278	12⟌2,436	8⟌2,768	16⟌347	3⟌173
3⟌2,580	8⟌432	12⟌144	9⟌819	5⟌1,752	8⟌416
16⟌1,664	18⟌2,250	4⟌3,412	19⟌361	38⟌344	9⟌512
13⟌3,302	3⟌6,150	19⟌8,550	12⟌420	45⟌287	21⟌7,413
8⟌439	13⟌3,413	9⟌373	15⟌870	2⟌6,910	14⟌2,439

Division Review II

Divide.

31$\overline{)624}$ 89$\overline{)3,156}$ 73$\overline{)5,411}$ 45$\overline{)7,135}$ 16$\overline{)864}$

72$\overline{)144}$ 23$\overline{)465}$ 63$\overline{)2,315}$ 76$\overline{)8,456}$ 12$\overline{)1295}$

12$\overline{)2,608}$ 24$\overline{)963}$ 13$\overline{)916}$ 11$\overline{)8,773}$ 27$\overline{)8,914}$

15$\overline{)135}$ 18$\overline{)6,108}$ 23$\overline{)1,115}$ 21$\overline{)845}$ 73$\overline{)356}$

46$\overline{)4,184}$ 57$\overline{)456}$ 20$\overline{)9,809}$ 26$\overline{)547}$ 19$\overline{)9,714}$

Reviewing dividing 3- and 4-digit dividends by 2-digit divisors

Mixed Review

1. Jack paid $29.75 for his new shoes. Grayson's cost $52.75. What is the ratio of Jack's shoes to Grayson's?

2. Finish Mary's book log. She reads seven books every three weeks.

Books	7					
Weeks	3	6	9	12	15	18

3. Joey has a bag containing 15 blue marbles, 19 red marbles, and 8 yellow marbles. If Joey pulls one marble out of the bag without looking, what is the probability that he will get a yellow marble on the first try?

   What is the probability that he will pull out a yellow marble on the second try (with one marble already removed)?

4. How many triangles are shown?

   How many right angles are there?_____

   How many obtuse angles are there?_____

   How many acute angles are there?_____

5. What kind of lines are these?

   ○ A. perpendicular
   ○ B. lines
   ○ C. intersecting lines
   ○ D. parallel

6. Which factors represent $3^3 \times 2^3 \times 5$?

   ○ A. $6 \times 9 \times 5$

   ○ B. $3 \times 2 \times 2 \times 2 \times 5$

   ○ C. $3 \times 3 \times 3 \times 2 \times 2 \times 2 \times 5$

   ○ D. 6×5

7. Multiply.

   $$\begin{array}{r} 1,238.83 \\ \times\ \ \ \ 4.00 \\ \hline \end{array}$$
   $$\begin{array}{r} 719.93 \\ \times\ 10.00 \\ \hline \end{array}$$

Fraction Review I

Add or subtract. Then simplify if you can. Circle the answers that are less than $\frac{1}{2}$.

$\frac{5}{8} - \frac{3}{8} =$

$\frac{16}{28} + \frac{9}{28} =$

$\frac{10}{20} - \frac{7}{20} =$

$\frac{7}{8} - \frac{3}{8} =$

$\frac{5}{16} + \frac{3}{16} =$

$\frac{11}{15} - \frac{8}{15} =$

$\frac{10}{14} - \frac{3}{14} =$

$\frac{16}{21} + \frac{2}{21} =$

$\frac{12}{15} - \frac{2}{15} =$

$\frac{7}{12} - \frac{2}{12} =$

$\frac{19}{20} - \frac{5}{20} =$

$\frac{11}{12} - \frac{7}{12} =$

$\frac{8}{13} + \frac{5}{13} =$

$\frac{9}{10} - \frac{7}{10} =$

$\frac{9}{12} + \frac{2}{12} =$

$\frac{6}{18} + \frac{8}{18} =$

$\frac{6}{7} - \frac{4}{7} =$

$\frac{8}{9} - \frac{2}{9} =$

$\frac{9}{16} + \frac{5}{16} =$

$\frac{32}{36} - \frac{18}{36} =$

$\frac{42}{45} - \frac{15}{45} =$

$\frac{9}{30} + \frac{15}{30} =$

$\frac{29}{30} - \frac{14}{30} =$

$\frac{30}{50} + \frac{15}{50} =$

Reviewing addition and subtraction of fractions with common denominators

Fraction Review II

Add or subtract.

$\frac{5}{6} + \frac{5}{8} = $ _____ $\frac{13}{21} + \frac{5}{7} = $ _____ $\frac{5}{6} + \frac{10}{18} = $ _____ $\frac{6}{7} + \frac{8}{9} = $ _____

$\frac{4}{5} + \frac{9}{15} = $ _____ $\frac{5}{16} + \frac{17}{8} = $ _____ $\frac{13}{12} + \frac{7}{8} = $ _____ $\frac{14}{24} + \frac{7}{12} = $ _____

$\frac{27}{30} - \frac{5}{6} = $ _____ $\frac{5}{6} - \frac{1}{5} = $ _____ $\frac{7}{8} - \frac{1}{2} = $ _____ $\frac{5}{6} - \frac{2}{9} = $ _____

$\frac{9}{16} - \frac{3}{8} = $ _____ $\frac{4}{5} - \frac{2}{8} = $ _____ $\frac{4}{7} - \frac{3}{14} = $ _____ $\frac{3}{4} - \frac{1}{5} = $ _____

$\frac{3}{6} - \frac{2}{15} = $ _____ $\frac{5}{8} - \frac{1}{6} = $ _____ $\frac{7}{9} - \frac{2}{6} = $ _____ $\frac{7}{24} - \frac{3}{12} = $ _____

$2\frac{1}{8} + 4\frac{1}{2} = $ _____ $3\frac{1}{2} + 5\frac{3}{6} = $ _____ $3\frac{9}{10} + 2\frac{4}{15} = $ _____ $2\frac{2}{3} + 3\frac{1}{6} = $ _____

$3\frac{7}{9} + 2\frac{3}{27} = $ _____ $4\frac{2}{8} + 3\frac{4}{16} = $ _____ $3\frac{2}{12} + 3\frac{1}{3} = $ _____ $6\frac{4}{9} + 2\frac{2}{3} = $ _____

$6\frac{7}{8} + \frac{2}{6} = $ _____ $6 + 3\frac{5}{9} = $ _____ $\frac{3}{12} + 5\frac{9}{12} = $ _____ $12\frac{4}{8} + \frac{2}{4} = $ _____

Compare. Use >, <, or =.

$5\frac{1}{4} - 1\frac{1}{8}$ ___ $5\frac{4}{6} - 1\frac{1}{3}$ $6\frac{5}{18} + 1\frac{3}{9}$ ___ $3\frac{1}{4} + 3\frac{4}{6}$ $\frac{6}{12}$ ___ $\frac{9}{24}$

$7\frac{1}{2} - 4$ ___ $9 - 7\frac{4}{10}$ $8\frac{7}{9} - 4\frac{1}{3}$ ___ $9\frac{5}{6} + 5\frac{2}{3}$ $\frac{10}{21}$ ___ $\frac{5}{7}$

$9 + 3\frac{4}{5}$ ___ $15 - 4\frac{2}{3}$ $9\frac{4}{10} + 2\frac{3}{5}$ ___ $10 + 3\frac{4}{9}$ $\frac{5}{15}$ ___ $\frac{2}{3}$

$7\frac{1}{4} - 2\frac{2}{8}$ ___ $3\frac{5}{8} - 1\frac{1}{3}$ $4\frac{7}{18} + 1\frac{3}{9}$ ___ $2\frac{1}{2} + 3\frac{1}{2}$ $\frac{3}{12}$ ___ $\frac{4}{8}$

Write the missing number.

$5\frac{2}{9} + $ ___ $= 11$ ___ $- 3\frac{2}{7} = 7\frac{5}{21}$ ___ $+ 2\frac{2}{3} = 5\frac{5}{6}$

___ $- 6\frac{3}{5} = 3\frac{1}{3}$ ___ $- 7\frac{1}{6} = 4\frac{2}{3}$ ___ $- 5\frac{3}{4} = 9\frac{5}{8}$

Reviewing addition and subtraction of fractions with unlike denominators

57

Fraction Review III

Multiply. Then simplify if you can.

$\frac{1}{3} \times \frac{5}{7} =$ _____ $\frac{2}{5} \times \frac{2}{6} =$ _____ $\frac{4}{8} \times \frac{5}{9} =$ _____ $\frac{5}{6} \times \frac{3}{4} =$ _____ $\frac{2}{8} \times \frac{4}{3} =$ _____

$\frac{3}{5} \times \frac{4}{9} =$ _____ $\frac{5}{4} \times \frac{1}{2} =$ _____ $\frac{7}{8} \times \frac{8}{9} =$ _____ $\frac{3}{9} \times \frac{7}{10} =$ _____ $\frac{5}{8} \times \frac{3}{4} =$ _____

$\frac{4}{9} \times 14 =$ _____ $\frac{7}{11} \times 9 =$ _____ $\frac{6}{9} \times 13 =$ _____ $22 \times \frac{1}{9} =$ _____ $\frac{2}{9} \times 18 =$ _____

$\frac{3}{12} \times \frac{1}{2} =$ _____ $\frac{2}{15} \times \frac{1}{2} =$ _____ $\frac{4}{9} \times \frac{5}{6} =$ _____ $\frac{4}{8} \times \frac{1}{2} =$ _____ $\frac{4}{11} \times \frac{4}{10} =$ _____

$\frac{4}{5} \times \frac{3}{9} =$ _____ $\frac{4}{12} \times \frac{5}{10} =$ _____ $\frac{7}{8} \times \frac{1}{4} =$ _____ $12 \times \frac{1}{9} =$ _____ $5 \times \frac{7}{12} =$ _____

Divide. Then simplify if you can.

$\frac{5}{9} \div \frac{1}{2} =$ _____ $\frac{4}{7} \div \frac{3}{4} =$ _____ $\frac{3}{7} \div \frac{5}{6} =$ _____ $\frac{8}{10} \div \frac{2}{9} =$ _____ $\frac{9}{12} \div \frac{1}{3} =$ _____

$\frac{3}{4} \div \frac{4}{6} =$ _____ $\frac{2}{9} \div \frac{5}{6} =$ _____ $\frac{3}{6} \div \frac{2}{9} =$ _____ $\frac{5}{14} \div \frac{1}{18} =$ _____ $10 \div \frac{3}{4} =$ _____

$\frac{8}{9} \div \frac{5}{7} =$ _____ $\frac{3}{12} \div \frac{7}{10} =$ _____ $\frac{4}{16} \div \frac{2}{3} =$ _____ $14 \div \frac{4}{5} =$ _____ $8 \div \frac{7}{9} =$ _____

$\frac{5}{13} \div \frac{3}{5} =$ _____ $\frac{7}{12} \div \frac{6}{10} =$ _____ $\frac{3}{5} \div \frac{3}{8} =$ _____ $\frac{12}{16} \div \frac{1}{2} =$ _____ $12 \div \frac{9}{10} =$ _____

$13 \div \frac{3}{11} =$ _____ $5 \div \frac{5}{18} =$ _____ $14 \div \frac{2}{7} =$ _____ $15 \div \frac{9}{16} =$ _____ $3 \div \frac{2}{3} =$ _____

Solve.

1. Allen wants to cut a board that is $6\frac{3}{4}$ feet long into $\frac{1}{2}$ foot sections. How many sections can he cut?

2. If Jackie runs $\frac{9}{10}$ of a mile every day, how many miles will she have run in two weeks?

   How many miles will she have run if she doubled the length of her daily run?

Mixed Review II

Solve the problems.

1. 739
   x 41

   ○ A. 30,299   ○ B. 31,299

   ○ C. 30,399   ○ D. 30,298

2. 1,209 ÷ 3 =   ○ A. 401   ○ B. 403

   ○ C. 404   ○ D. 405

3. Kenny and Joe caught a total of 18 fish. Kenny caught six more fish than Joe. How many fish did each of them catch?

4. Find the mean of the numbers 94, 96, 98, 76, 84, 86, 82, and 88.

   ○ A. 83   ○ B. 88   ○ C. 92   ○ D. 90

5. Look at each number. Write P if it is prime and C if it is composite.

21 ____	55 ____	29 ____
11 ____	12 ____	17 ____
27 ____	41 ____	15 ____
36 ____	39 ____	52 ____
48 ____	47 ____	85 ____

6. Divide.

   $3.2\overline{)12.8}$ $6.8\overline{)29.24}$

7. Find the least common multiple.

   8 and 16 = _____   5 and 15 = _____

   3 and 7 = _____   12 and 8 = _____

   18 and 9 = _____   30 and 5 = _____

   12 and 36 = _____   6 and 9 = _____

8. Round to the nearest thousand.

   26,076 _____   3,45 _____

   187,093 _____   20,897 _____

   9,641 _____   127,679 _____

   2,931 _____   10,769 _____

9. Write each mixed numeral as a decimal.

   $3\frac{1}{4}$ = _____ $2\frac{3}{5}$ = _____

   $2\frac{7}{20}$ = _____ $4\frac{1}{5}$ = _____

   $3\frac{3}{8}$ = _____ $6\frac{21}{40}$ = _____

   $4\frac{9}{25}$ = _____ $3\frac{14}{50}$ = _____

   $8\frac{7}{8}$ = _____ $10\frac{11}{50}$ = _____

10. Write each decimal as a fraction.

    0.8 = _____   0.6 = _____

    0.08 = _____   0.55 = _____

    4.6 = _____   4.5 = _____

    5.15 = _____   4.75 = _____

    0.004 = _____   3.8 = _____

Applying math skills

59

Mixed Review III

Solve the problems.

1. Which group of numbers are evenly divisible by 2?

   ○ A. 341 and 845　　○ B. 1001 and 123
   ○ C. 126 and 628　　○ D. 653 and 63

2.
7 ft. 9 in.	1 yd. 2 ft.
12 ft. 7 in.	1 yd. 1 ft.
+ 3 ft. 10 in.	+ 2 yd. 1 ft.

3. $\frac{4}{5} \div \frac{3}{4} =$

   ○ A. $2\frac{1}{15}$　　○ B. $1\frac{2}{15}$

   ○ C. $1\frac{1}{15}$　　○ D. $\frac{17}{15}$

4. Write the square of each number.

   9^2　　20^2　　32^2　　65^2　　14^2

   ___　___　___　___　___

5. Change each fraction to percents.

   $\frac{7}{20}$ = _____

   $\frac{4}{5}$ = _____

   $\frac{7}{8}$ = _____

6.
$8\frac{5}{8}$	$3\frac{5}{6}$	$7\frac{3}{4}$
$-1\frac{1}{4}$	$-1\frac{2}{3}$	$-4\frac{3}{8}$

7. Write the value of each.

   $10^3 =$　　　$3^3 =$　　　$8^4 =$

   $10^2 =$　　　$2^5 =$　　　$9^4 =$

   $10^5 =$　　　$6^3 =$　　　$7^3 =$

8.
3 ft. $2\frac{1}{3}$ in.	6 yd. 8 in.
x　　8	x　　4

4 yd. 2 ft.	9 yd. 9 in.
x　　3	x　　4

9. Which shows a translation of the △ ?

   ○ A.　　　○ B.

   ○ C.　　　○ D.

10. $\frac{5}{6} \times \frac{3}{5} =$

    ○ A. $\frac{1}{3}$　　○ B. $\frac{18}{30}$

    ○ C. $\frac{1}{8}$　　○ D. $\frac{1}{2}$

Answer Key

Please take time to review the work your child has completed and remember to praise both success and effort. If your child makes a mistake, let him or her know that mistakes are a part of learning. Then explain the correct answer and how to find it. Taking the time to help your child and an active interest in his or her progress shows that you feel learning is important.

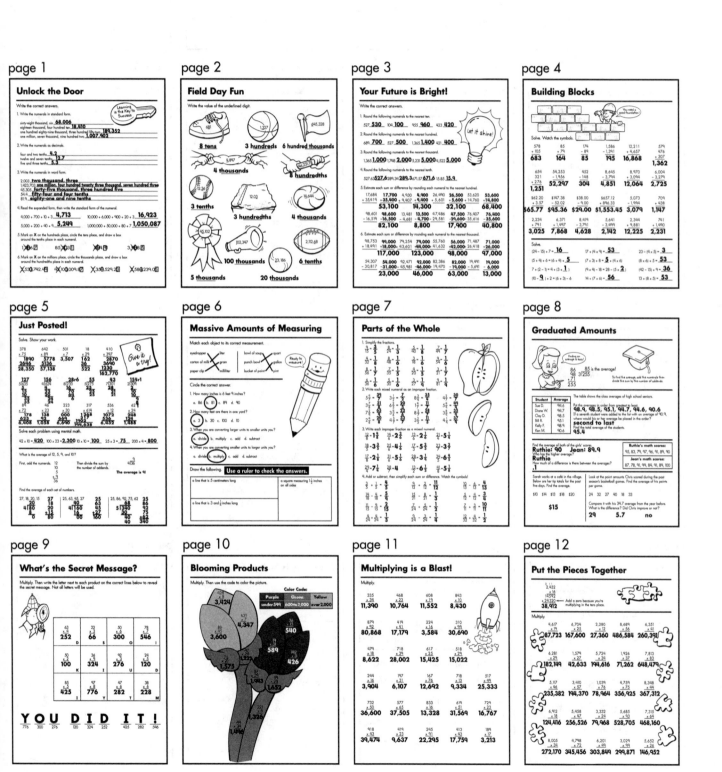

Multiply Three by Three

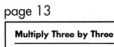

```
  263
× 146
 1578   — Add a zero because you're multiplying in the tens place.
10520
26300   — Add two zeros because you're multiplying in the hundreds place.
38398
```

Multiply.

126 × 158 = **19,908**	325 × 122 = **39,650**	401 × 241 = **96,641**	836 × 425 = **355,300**	406 × 134 = **54,404**
227 × 114 = **25,878**	531 × 289 = **153,459**	200 × 146 = **29,200**	637 × 741 = **472,017**	342 × 300 = **102,600**
476 × 220 = **104,720**	512 × 478 = **244,736**	339 × 157 = **53,223**	741 × 335 = **248,235**	874 × 209 = **182,666**
986 × 608 = **599,488**	678 × 385 = **261,030**	425 × 227 = **96,475**	507 × 775 = **265,668**	805 × 775 = **623,875**

Make a Match

Divide. Then draw a line to the matching quotients.

Keep it Up, Up, Up!

Divide.

52r8	55r10	75r5
65r9	22r3	
16r16	21r31	21r22	37r9	37r3
21	21r6	21r14	14r10	61r8
32r16	62r13	25r4	42r1	24r16
39r13	48r9	43r17	25r32	29r15

Crack the Code

At which store did the dog lose its tail?

r e - t a i l

s h o p !

Division Skills are Blooming!

Divide.

The Grocery Hang Out

Read each problem then divide or multiply to solve it.

1. **$3.75**
2. **$.51**
3. **240**
4. **$7.50**
5. **$5.00**
6. **225**

Mean, Median, Mode

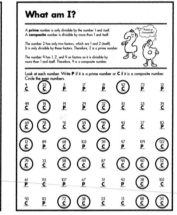

Find the mean, median, and mode for each.

Basketball Points		
Mean: **19**	Median: **19**	Mode: **none**

Golf Scores		
Mean: **81**	Median: **82.5**	Mode: **90**

Data	mean	median	mode
10, 17, 10, 14, 19	14	14	10
18, 19, 64, 19, 32, 60, 61	39	32	19
11, 38, 13, 38, 40	28	38	38
12, 15, 11, 15, 12, 10, 15	13	13	15
87, 88, 95, 79, 83, 79	84	82	79
96, 62, 97, 100, 96, 87, 85	89	96	96

What am I?

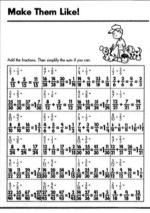

Look at each number. Write **P** if it is a prime number or **C** if it is a composite number. Circle the even numbers.

Action Fractions

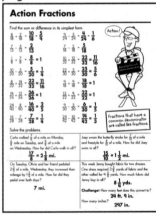

Find the sum or difference in its simplest form.

Solve the problems.

Carla walked... **17/12 = 2 1/4 mi.**

Joey swam... **9/8 = 1 1/8 mi.**

On Tuesday, Olivia... **7 mi.**

This week Jenny... **8 1/4 yds.**

Challenge: **24 ft. 9 in.**

How many inches? **297 in.**

What Do We Have in Common?

Find the LCM/LCD for each pair fractions and convert to like fractions.

Simple Comparisons

Convert to like fractions, then compare using the symbols >, =, or <. Circle each fraction whose value is greater than 1.

Convert to like fractions, then put them in order from least to greatest.

Make Them Like!

Add the fractions. Then simplify the sum if you can.

Simple Subtraction with Fractions

Subtract the fractions. Then simplify the difference if you can.

Picking Up The Pace!

Solve the problems.

Everything is Multiplying!

Multiply the fractions. Then simplify the product if you can.

Multiplying by Fractions

Multiply.

What is 1/9 of 45? **5**
What is 1/4 of 16? **4**
What is 1/4 of 20? **5**
What is 1/4 of 4? **1 1/2**
What is 1/5 of 8? **1 3/5**
What is 1/8 of 26? **3 1/4**

Answers

page 29

Flipping over Division

Divide the fractions. Show your work.

$\frac{2}{3} \div \frac{1}{5} = \frac{2}{3} \times \frac{5}{1} = \frac{10}{3} = 3\frac{1}{3}$ (answers as shown)

(division of fractions worksheet with worked answers)

page 30

Fruity Fractions

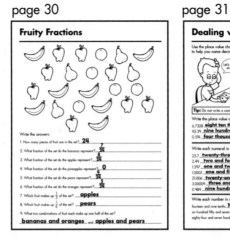

Write the answers.

1. How many pieces of fruit are in the set? **24**
2. What fraction of the set do the bananas represent? **7/24**
3. What fraction of the set do the apples represent? **7/24**
4. What fraction of the set do the pineapples represent? **0**
5. What fraction of the set do the oranges represent? **5/24**
6. What fraction of the set do the pears represent? **5/24**
7. Which fruit makes up 1/3 of the set? **apples**
8. Which fruit makes up 1/4 of the set? **pears**
9. What two combinations of fruit each make up half of the set?
bananas and oranges and **apples and pears**

page 31

Dealing with Decimals

Use the place value chart at the right to help you name decimal values.

The number 217.5344 is read as "two hundred seventeen and five thousand, three hundred ninety-four ten-thousandths."

Tip: Do not write a comma between place values for the numerals after the decimal point.

Write the place value of the last digit in each number.

6.7328 **eight ten thousandths**   4.345 **five thousandths**
43.39 **nine hundredths**   2.43893 **three hundred thousandths**
0.594 **four thousandths**   13.81573 **three hundred thousandths**

Write each numeral in written form. Don't forget to use "and."

23.7 **twenty-three and seven tenths**
2.49 **two and forty-nine hundredths**
1.297 **one and two hundred ninety-seven thousandths**
10.005 **ten and five ten thousandths**
21.006 **twenty-one and six thousandths**
3.00009 **three and nine hundred thousandths**
0.984 **nine hundred eighty-four thousandths**

Write each number in standard form.

fourteen and nine tenths **14.9**   nine and ten thousandths **9.010**
six hundred fifty and seven ten thousandths **650.007**   ninety-one and four tenths **91.004**
eighty-four and seven hundredths **84.07**   one and nine millionths **1.000009**

page 32

Decimal Double Take

The same amount can be written as a fraction or a decimal.
.6 is also 6/10

Write the correct letters to match the fractions and decimals.

34/100 **D**   83/100 **P**   61/100 **N**
.57 **K**   .5 **Q**   .01 **O**
42/100 **I**   50/100 **C**   .83 **P**
60/100 **A**   .34 **D**   .001 **Q**
.79 **Q**   64 **X**   .1 **R**
34/1000 **F**   .79 **Q**   57/1000 **T**
41/100 **M**   .79 **M**   .33 **T**
27/100 **L**   114/100 **V**   .9 **Y**
.48 **F**   33/100 **T**   .114 **V**
29/100 **H**   .341 **J**   .08 **W**
.2 **E**   57/1000 **K**   .64 **X**
.7 **J**   .61 **U**   .512 **Z**
.54 **C**   61 **L**

page 33

Get the Point?

To change a percent to a decimal, move the decimal point two places to the left and drop the percent sign.
44% = .44

Change each percent to a decimal.

90% = **.9**   48% = **.48**   28% = **.28**   29% = **.29**   3% = **.03**
12% = **.12**   64% = **.64**   79% = **.79**   24% = **.24**   .3% = **.003**
5% = **.05**   56% = **.56**   94% = **.94**   .2% = **.2**   27% = **.27**
17% = **.17**   19% = **.19**   82% = **.82**   .3% = **.03**   72% = **.72**
26% = **.26**   10% = **.1**   78% = **.78**   99% = **.99**   41% = **.41**
9% = **.09**   4% = **.04**   .14% = **.14**   36% = **.36**   6% = **.06**

Complete the table.

Fractions	Decimals	Percents
1/2	0.5	**50%**
1/5	**.2**	20%
625/100	0.625	62.5%
1/10	**.1**	**10%**
69/100	0.69	69%

page 34

Rule of Thumb

Add.

When adding or subtracting decimals, always line up the decimal points!

(addition problems with answers)
15.914   29.66   48.957
44.175   23.267   21.527
97.177   592.7935   1,141.113   30.879   36.5194   24.3318
27.116   58.68   28.5044   76.7923   103.102   97.904

Line up the decimals and solve. (Hint: Write the problems vertically.)

5.8001 + 41.9 = **47.7001**   .985 + 2.0008 = **2.9158**   0.3 + .00078 = **.30078**
0.54 + 8.0040 = **8.544**   4.5 + 12.7088 = **17.2088**   3.4 + 0.0012 = **3.4012**

page 35

Falling Amounts

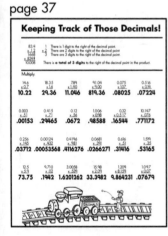

Subtract.

14.039   4.292   .083
18.408   11.5495   28.293
46.146   .7926   .0078   1.388   5.64   .77
6.02   4.54149   4.779   7.30241   7.851   .393

Line up the decimals and solve. (Hint: Write the problems vertically!)

30.03 - .49 = **5.54**   23.7 - 4.092 = **19.608**   14.907 - 0.989 = **13.918**
3.410 - .891 = **2.519**   12 - 0.0189 = **11.9811**   7.410 - 0.59 = **6.82**

page 36

Little Makes BIG!

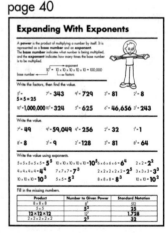

Prime factorization is writing a composite number as a product of prime factors.

To find the prime factorization of 24, only use prime numbers as factors to equal 24.

Look! These numbers are prime! $2 \times 2 \times 2 \times 3$
$4 \times 3 = 24$

Draw a line to match the number to its factorization. (Hint: The answers must be entirely in prime numbers.)

(matching section)

Write the prime factorization for the following numbers.

28 **2 × 2 × 7**   72 **2 × 2 × 2 × 3 × 3**
16 **2 × 2 × 2 × 2**   144 **2 × 2 × 2 × 2 × 3 × 3**
21 **3 × 7**   56 **2 × 2 × 2 × 7**
18 **2 × 3 × 3**   32 **2 × 2 × 2 × 2 × 2**
27 **3 × 3 × 3**   42 **2 × 3 × 7**

Find the product.

3 × 5 × 5 × 11 = **825**   2 × 3 × 3 = **18**   2 × 2 × 2 × 3 × 3 = **72**
2 × 2 × 3 × 3 × 5 = **180**   3 × 7 × 7 = **147**   2 × 2 × 5 = **20**

page 37

Keeping Track of Those Decimals!

There is 1 digit to the right of the decimal point.
There are 2 digits to the right of the decimal point.
There are 3 digits to the right of the decimal point.

There is a **total** of 3 digits to the right of the decimal point in the product.

Multiply.

10.22   29.36   11.046   814.36   .08025   .07224
.00153   .29465   .0672   .98588   .16544   .771172
.03712   .00053568   .4116276   .0266271   .31416   .53165
73.75   .1942   1.6201262   33.3982   9.864231   .07679

page 38

Razzle Dazzle Decimals

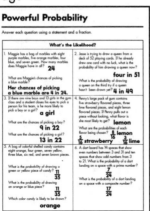

Divide.

1.3   1.08   2.43   7.5   11.1   .91
4.5   .75   .93   4.61   20.54   2.21
8.3   .2   1344   .73   7.9   3.9
1.47   4.935   3.95   3.2   4   8.9
8.15   6.4   .74   4.525   .4   1.15
33.15   4.84   8.1   6.025   1.2

page 39

Exploring Decimal Division

First, convert the divisor into a whole number by multiplying the divisor and dividend by 10.

Next, place the decimal point in the quotient and divide as with whole numbers.

Divide.

.7   1.6   28   850   35
8.3   .2   1344   .73   7.9   3.9
.51   7.4   6.12   6.32   30   .521
6.25   4.2   7.6   .64   1260   1.55

page 40

Expanding With Exponents

A **power** is the product of multiplying a number by itself. It is represented as a **base number** and an **exponent**. The **base number** indicates what number is being multiplied, and the **exponent** indicates how many times the base number is to be multiplied.

$10^5 = 10 \times 10 \times 10 \times 10 \times 10 = 100,000$

Write the factors, then find the value.

$5^2 =$ **25** $7^3 =$ **343** $9^3 =$ **729** $3^4 =$ **81** $2^3 =$ **8**
$5 \times 5 = 25$
$10^6 =$ **1,000,000** $18^2 =$ **324** $5^4 =$ **625** $6^3 =$ **46,656** $3^5 =$ **243**

Write the value.

$7^2 =$ **49** $9^4 =$ **59,049** $4^4 =$ **256** $2^5 =$ **32** $1^6 =$ **1**
$8^2 =$ **64** $3^2 =$ **9** $2^7 =$ **128** $3^4 =$ **81** $2^6 =$ **64**

Write the value using exponents.

$5 \times 5 \times 5 \times 5 \times 5 =$ **5⁵** $10 \times 10 \times 10 \times 10 \times 10 =$ **10⁵** $6 \times 6 \times 6 \times 6 =$ **6⁴** $2 \times 2 =$ **2²**
$10 \times 10 \times 10 =$ **10³** $5 \times 5 =$ **5²** $8 \times 8 \times 8 =$ **8³** $10 \times 10 =$ **10²**

Fill in the missing numbers.

Product	Number to Given Power	Standard Notation
8 × 8 × 8	8^3	512
5 × 5	5^2	25
12 × 12 × 12	12^3	1,728
2 × 2 × 2 × 2 × 2	2^5	32

page 41

Slurping Down Cubes and Squares

The **square** of a number is the number times itself.
$5^2 = 5 \times 5 = 25$

The **cube** of a number is the number multiplied twice by itself.
$5^3 = 5 \times 5 \times 5 = 125$

Write the square or cube of each number.

$4^2 =$ **4 × 4 = 16** $9^2 =$ **81** $3^3 =$ **27**
$6^3 =$ **216** $7^2 =$ **49** $15^3 =$ **3,375**
$10^3 =$ **1,000** $5^3 =$ **125** $14^2 =$ **196**
$20^2 =$ **400** $24^3 =$ **13,824** $6^4 =$ **6,854**
$8^3 =$ **512** $13^2 =$ **169** $48^2 =$ **2,304**
$17^2 =$ **289** $25^3 =$ **15,625** $37^2 =$ **1,369**

Write the square root.

36 = **6**   64 = **8**   81 = **9**   25 = **5**   324 = **18**   529 = **23**
400 = **20**   225 = **15**   625 = **25**   144 = **12**   900 = **30**   2,500 = **50**

Write the cube root.

512 = **8³**   1,000 = **10³**   64 = **4³**   27 = **3³**   8 = **2³**   216 = **6³**
512 = **8³**   1,728 = **12³**   2,744 = **14³**   343 = **7³**   8,000 = **20³**   6,859 = **19³**

page 42

Powerful Probability

Answer each question using a statement and a fraction.

What's the Likelihood?

1. Maggie has a bag containing eight purple marbles, five orange marbles, four blue, and seven green. How many marbles does Maggie have in all? **24**
What is Maggie's chances of picking a blue marble? **four in 24**
Her chances of picking a blue marble are 4 in 24.

2. If there are nine boys and 13 girls in the gym class and a student closes his eyes to pick a person for his team, is he more likely to pick a boy or a girl? **a girl**
What are the chances of picking a boy? **9 in 22**
What are the chances of picking a girl? **13 in 22**

3. A bag of colorful shelled candy contains eight orange, four green, seven yellow, three blue, six red, and seven brown pieces.
What is the probability of drawing a green or yellow piece of candy? **11/35**
What is the probability of drawing an orange or blue piece? **11/35**
Which color candy is likely to be drawn? **orange**

4. Jesse is trying to draw a queen from a deck of 52 playing cards. If he already drew one card with no luck, what is the probability of him drawing a queen now? **four in 51**
What is the probability of drawing a queen on the third try if a queen hasn't been drawn yet? **4 in 49**

5. Penny's large pack of gum contains five strawberry flavored pieces, three lime flavored pieces, and eight lemon flavored pieces. If Penny pulls out a piece without looking, what flavor is she most likely to get? **lemon**
What are the probabilities of each flavor being chosen? **5/16 strawberry   8/16 lemon   3/16 lime**

6. A dart board has 14 spaces that show even numbers between 3 and 31 and ten spaces that show odd numbers from 3 to 21. What is the probability of a dart landing on a space with a prime number? **11/24**
What is the probability of a dart landing on a space with a composite number? **17/24**

page 43

Terrific Tables

Complete each rate table, then answer the questions.

Mr. Petz has a chicken farm. He is able to collect 60 dozen eggs per week from his chickens.

Dozen	60	120	180	240	300	360	420	480	540	600
Week										

How many dozen eggs does Mr. Petz collect in a six-week period? **360 dozen eggs**
If there are four weeks in a month, how many dozen eggs are collected in two months? **480 dozen eggs**
How many dozen eggs are collected in a three-month period? **720 dozen eggs**

Dean is taking a trip. His car will travel 30 miles per gallon of gasoline on the highway.

Miles	30	60	90	120	150	180	210	240	270	300
Gallons		2	3	4	5	6	7	8	9	10

How far can the car travel on eight gallons of gasoline? **240 miles**
If Dean went 270 miles, how many gallons of gas did he use? **9 gallons**
If the tank in Dean's car is completely full of gas at 15 gallons, how far can he go on one tank of gas? **450 miles**

The Pampered Pet Groomers can groom up to 18 dogs in a two-day period.

Pets	18	36	54	72	90	108	126	144	162	180
Days	2	4	6	8	10	12	14	16	18	20

How many dogs can be groomed in a two-week period? **126 dogs**
If there are 30 days in this month, how many pets can be groomed in the month? **270 dogs**
If two groomers do all the grooming, how many dogs can one groomer take care of in a ten-day period? **45 dogs**

page 44

Mix and Match Geometry

Write the correct letters to match the geometric terms to their definitions.

Quadrilateral **B**
Parallelogram **F**
Point **A**
Right Angle **G**
Acute angle **I**
Obtuse angle **H**
Line **E**
Decagon **D**
Congruent **J**
Octagon **C**
Pentagon **K**
Heptagon **S**
Nonagon **P**
Dodecagon **O**
Hexagon **M**
Rotation **R**
Translation **Q**
Reflection **T**
Parallel **L**
Perpendicular **N**

A) part of a line between two end points, an exact location
B) a polygon with four sides
C) a polygon with eight sides
D) a ten-sided polygon
E) a never-ending path in the opposite direction with no endpoints
F) a quadrilateral whose opposite sides are parallel and congruent
G) a 90° angle
H) an angle more than 90°
I) an angle less than 90°
J) having the same size and shape
K) a polygon with five sides and angles
L) two line segments that are exactly the same distance apart
M) a polygon with six sides and angles
N) two lines that intersect to form four right angles
O) a polygon with twelve sides and angles
P) a polygon with nine sides and angles
Q) sliding a figure in any direction
R) turning a figure around a point
S) a polygon with seven sides and angles
T) when a figure is flipped over a line

page 45

What's My Name?

A triangle has three names. The last name is always "triangle."

The 1st name is from the angle:
Any triangle with a 90° angle is a right triangle.
Any triangle with an angle less than 90° is an acute triangle.
Any triangle with an angle greater than 90° is an obtuse triangle.

The 2nd name is from the sides:
If all sides are equal, the triangle is equilateral.
If only two sides are equal, the triangle is isosceles.
If no sides are equal, the triangle is scalene.

Write the three-word name for each triangle.

acute isosceles triangle | right isosceles triangle | obtuse isosceles triangle
obtuse isosceles triangle | right scalene triangle | right scalene triangle
acute isosceles triangle | right isosceles triangle | right scalene triangle

Challenge yourself!
How many combinations of triangles can there be?

Find the angles listed. Write the letters that form these angles.

Example: ECF is an acute angle.

Two right angles: **GCB, GCD**

Two obtuse angles: **FCD, ECD**

Five acute angles: **ECB, FCE, FCB, ECG, FCG**

page 46

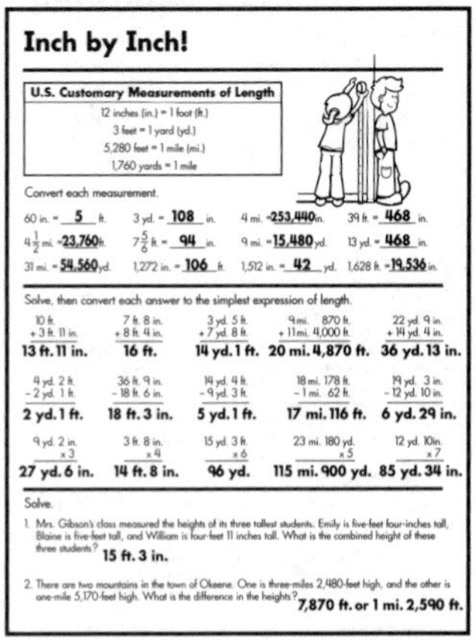

Inch by Inch!

U.S. Customary Measurements of Length
12 inches (in.) = 1 foot (ft.)
3 feet = 1 yard (yd.)
5,280 feet = 1 mile (mi.)
1,760 yards = 1 mile

Convert each measurement.

60 in. = **5** ft.   3 ft. = **108** in.   4 mi. = **253,440** in.   39 ft. = **468** in.
4½ ft. = **23,760** in.   7½ ft. = **94** in.   3 mi. = **15,840** yd.   13 yd. = **468** in.
31 mi. = **54,560** yd.   1,272 in. = **106** ft.   1,512 in. = **42** yd.   1,628 ft. = **19,536** in.

Solve, then convert each answer to the simplest expression of length.

13 ft. 11 in.   16 ft.   14 yd. 1 ft. 20 mi. 4,870 ft. 36 yd. 13 in.

2 yd. 1 ft.   18 ft. 3 in.   5 yd. 1 ft.   17 mi. 116 ft.   6 yd. 29 in.

27 yd. 6 in.   14 ft. 8 in.   96 yd.   115 mi. 900 yd. 85 yd. 34 in.

Solve.

1. Mrs. Gibson's class measured the heights of its three tallest students. Emily is five-feet four-inches tall, Blaine is five-feet tall, and William is four-feet 11 inches tall. What is the combined height of these three students? **15 ft. 3 in.**

2. There are two mountains in the town of Okeene. One is three-miles 2,480-feet high, and the other is one-mile 5,170-feet high. What is the difference in the heights? **7,870 ft. or 1 mi. 2,590 ft.**

page 47

Massive Amounts of Measurement

U.S. Customary Measurements of Liquid	U.S. Customary Measurements of Weight
1 pint (pt.) = 2 cups (c.)	16 ounces (oz.) = 1 pound (lb.)
1 quart (qt.) = 2 pints	2,000 pounds = 1 ton (T.)
1 gallon (gal.) = 4 quarts	

Write the correct unit of measure.

a small juice box drink 1 **pt.**   a mouse weighs 4 **oz.**
a basketball weighs 28 **lb.**   a bicycle weighs 28 **lb.**
a truck weighs 2 **T.**   a container of yogurt holds 1 **pt.**
a horse trailer weighs 1 **T.**   an apple weighs 90 **oz.**
a bag of potatoes weighs 5 **lb.**   a swimming pool holds 1,200 **gal.**
a set of pens weighs 4 **oz.**   a flashlight weighs 2 **lb.**
a compact disc weighs 4 **oz.**
a washing machine holds 15 **gal.**   clothes in the washing machine weigh 20 **lb.**

Convert each measurement.

6 qt. = **24** c.   9 pt. = **18** c.   3 gal. = **48** c.   14 qt. = **56** c.
16 gal. = **128** pt.   23 qt. = **46** pt.   50 gal. = **800** pt.   36 qt. = **72** pt.
96 oz. = **6** lb.   132 lb. = **2,112** oz.   18 lb. = **288** oz.   3 T. = **6,000** lb.
1.8 T. = **57,600** oz.   48 oz. = **3** lb.   11½ lb. = **32,256** oz.   4,000 lb. = **2** T.
9 gal. = **272** pt.   4,000 pt. = **16,000** c.   346 lb. = **5,536** oz.   561 qt. = **1,122** pt.

page 48

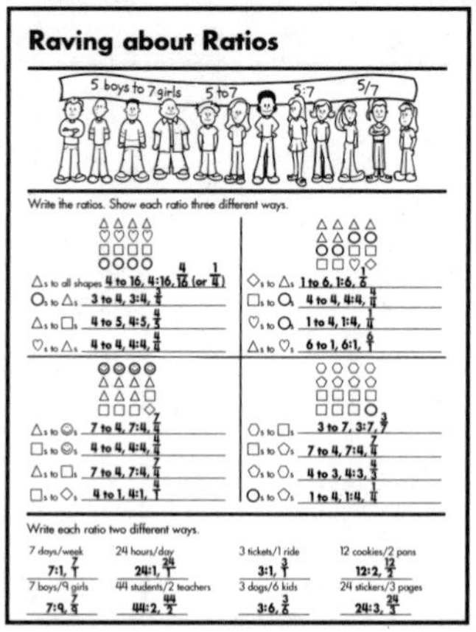

Raving about Ratios

5 boys to 7 girls   5 to 7   5:7   5/7

Write the ratios. Show each ratio three different ways.

△s to all shapes: **4 to 16, 4:16, 4/16 (or ¼)**   □s to △s: **4 to 6, 4:6, 4/6**
○s to △s: **3 to 4, 3:4, ¾**   □s to ○s: **4 to 3, 4:3, 4/3**
♡s to △s: **4 to 4, 4:4, 4/4**   ♡s to □s: **4 to 4, 4:4, 4/4**

△s to □s: **7 to 4, 7:4, 7/4**   ○s to □s: **3 to 7, 3:7, 3/7**
△s to ○s: **7 to 4, 7:4, 7/4**   ♡s to △s: **4 to 3, 4:3, 4/3**
△s to ♡s: **7 to 4, 7:4, 7/4**   △s to ♡s: **4 to 1, 4:1, 4/1**

Write each ratio two different ways.

7 days/week: **7/1, 7:1**   24 hours/day: **24/1, 24:1**   3 tickets/1 ride: **3/1, 3:1**   12 cookies/2 pans: **12/2, 12:2**
7 boys/9 girls: **7/9, 7:9**   44 students/2 teachers: **44/2, 44:2**   36/6 kids: **36/6, 36:6**   24 stickers/3 pages: **24/3, 24:3**

page 49

Powerful Percents

Let's change the fraction to a percent.

1st: Change the fraction to a decimal.

Divide the numerator by the denominator.
Add 0's to keep from having a remainder.

2nd: Move the decimal point two places to the right and add the percent sign.

Change each fraction to a percent. Don't forget the percent sign.

80/100 = **80%**   ¾ = **75%**   ⅜ = **37.50%**   9/10 = **90%**   3/19 = **16%**
22/100 = **22%**   ⅘ = **80%**   9/20 = **45%**   4/25 = **16%**   9/100 = **9%**
⅗ = **60%**   6/25 = **24%**   ⅔ = **46%**   16/25 = **64%**   ⅞ = **88%**
11/20 = **55%**   2/25 = **8%**   8/15 = **53%**   3/10 = **30%**   ⅖ = **40%**
8/25 = **32%**   11/50 = **22%**   23/25 = **92%**   9/25 = **36%**   ⅕ = **20%**

Challenge yourself!
See how many things you can list that express percents. For example, test scores come in percents.

Answers will vary.

page 50

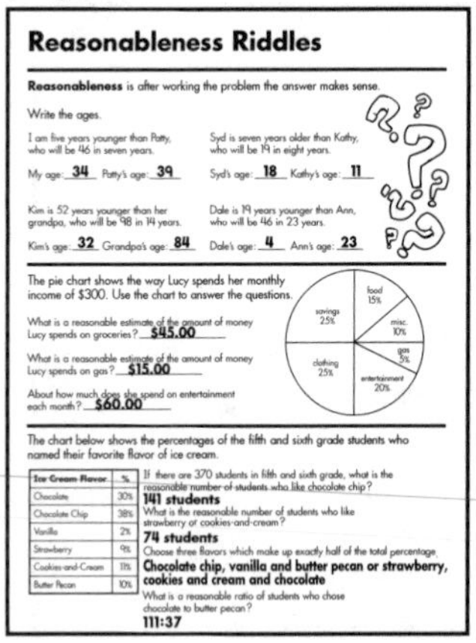

Reasonableness Riddles

Reasonableness is after working the problem the answer makes sense.

Write the ages.

I am five years younger than Patty, who will be 46 in seven years.   Syd is seven years older than Kathy, who will be 14 in eight years.

My age: **34**   Patty's age: **39**   Syd's age: **18**   Kathy's age: **11**

Kim is 52 years younger than her grandpa, who will be 98 in 14 years.   Dale is 14 years younger than Ann, who will be 16 in 23 years.

Kim's age: **32**   Grandpa's age: **84**   Ann's age: **70**   Dale's age: **9**

The pie chart shows the way Lucy spends her monthly income of $300. Use the chart to answer the questions.

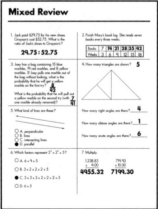

What is a reasonable estimate of the amount of money Lucy spends on groceries? **$45.00**

What is a reasonable estimate of the amount of money Lucy spends on her car? **$15.00**

About how much does she spend on entertainment each month? **$60.00**

The chart below shows the percentages of the fifth and sixth grade students who named their favorite flavor of ice cream.

Ice Cream Flavor	%
Chocolate	20%
Chocolate Chip	18%
Vanilla	7%
Strawberry	10%
Cookies-and-Cream	35%
Butter Pecan	10%

If there are 370 students in fifth and sixth grade, what is the reasonable number of students who like chocolate chip? **141 students**

What is the reasonable number of students who like strawberry or cookies-and-cream? **74 students**

Choose three flavors which make up exactly half of the total percentage. **Chocolate chip, vanilla and butter pecan or strawberry, cookies and cream and chocolate**

What is a reasonable ratio of students who chose chocolate to butter pecan? **111:37**

page 51

Multiplication Review I

Multiply.

162 × 65 = **10,530**   215 × 84 = **18,060**   165 × 66 = **10,890**   932 × 73 = **68,036**   198 × 23 = **4,554**   462 × 65 = **30,030**

198 × 73 = **14,454**   1,462 × 30 = **43,860**   2,432 × 23 = **55,936**   1,665 × 79 = **131,535**   3,913 × 77 = **301,301**   174 × 36 = **6,264**

173 × 72 = **12,456**   1,643 × 65 = **106,745**   345 × 44 = **15,180**   415 × 46 = **19,090**   654 × 73 = **47,742**   3,346 × 94 = **314,524**

354 × 13 = **4,602**   982 × 70 = **68,740**   491 × 43 = **21,113**   2,651 × 63 = **167,013**   1,531 × 61 = **93,391**   9,874 × 75 = **740,925**

6,462 × 36 = **232,632**   5,913 × 85 = **395,149**   5,499 × 54 = **513,346**   879 × 83 = **72,957**   563 × 61 = **34,343**   163 × 39 = **6,357**

9,963 × 43 = **428,409**   4,563 × 61 = **278,343**   428 × 63 = **26,964**   521 × 42 = **23,177**   1,569 × 96 = **150,624**   255 × 50 = **12,750**

page 52

Multiplication Review II

Multiply.

654 × 865 = **565,710**   166 × 188 = **31,208**   235 × 365 = **85,775**   167 × 973 = **162,491**   933 × 425 = **396,525**   741 × 104 = **77,064**

199 × 371 = **73,829**   465 × 230 = **106,950**   432 × 796 = **343,872**   665 × 123 = **81,795**   923 × 679 = **626,717**   827 × 427 = **353,129**

173 × 721 = **124,733**   643 × 986 = **298,945**   346 × 446 = **154,316**   411 × 125 = **51,375**   654 × 733 = **479,382**   963 × 783 = **754,630**

354 × 123 = **43,542**   982 × 873 = **221,932**   497 × 376 = **186,872**   6,651 × 569 = **3,784,419**   2,531 × 331 = **837,761**   748 × 873 = **653,004**

462 × 256 = **118,272**   531 × 257 = **136,467**   874 × 733 = **368,629**   879 × 733 = **644,307**   674 × 69 = **46,592**   226 × 462 = **104,412**

page 53

Division Review I

Divide.

6)240 = **40**   2)5,436 = **2718**   35)5,257 = **150r7**   6)1,224 = **204**   4)573 = **143r1**   3)256 = **85r3**

3)7,564 = **2521r1**   9)1,278 = **142**   12)2,436 = **203**   16)547 = **346**   3)635 = **21r11**   3)173 = **57r2**

3)2,580 = **860**   8)432 = **54**   9)144 = **12**   5)752 = **91**   3)... = **350r2**   6)... = **52**

6)1,664 = **104**   8)2,230 = **125**   4)1,412 = **853**   14)361 = **19**   3)... = **9r2**   3)... = **56r8**

13)3,302 = **254**   3)6,150 = **2050**   14)6,350 = **450**   12)... = **35**   45)287 = **6r17**   2)... = **353**

8)439 = **54r7**   3)1,343 = **262r7**   2)... = **41r4**   15)870 = **58**   2)6,910 = **3455**   14)2,439 = **174r3**

page 54

Division Review II

Divide.

31)624 = **20r4**   84)3,156 = **35r41**   73)5,411 = **74r9**   45)7,135 = **158r25**   16)864 = **54**

72)144 = **2**   23)465 = **20r5**   63)2,315 = **36r47**   76)8,456 = **111r20**   12)1,295 = **107r11**

12)2,608 = **217r4**   24)963 = **40r3**   12)846 = **70r6**   11)8,773 = **797r6**   27)8,914 = **330r4**

15)135 = **9**   18)6,108 = **339r6**   23)1,115 = **48r11**   21)845 = **40r5**   73)356 = **4r4**

46)4,184 = **90r44**   57)456 = **8**   20)9,804 = **490r9**   26)547 = **21r1**   14)7,674 = **511r5**

page 55

Mixed Review

1. Jack paid $29.75 for his new shoes. Grayson's cost $52.75. What is the ratio of Jack's shoes to Grayson's? **29.75 : 52.75**

2. Finish Mary's book log. She reads seven books every three weeks.

Books	7	14	21	28	35	42
Weeks	3	6	9	12	15	18

3. Joey has a bag containing 15 blue marbles, 14 red marbles, and 8 yellow marbles. If you pulled one marble out of the bag without looking, what is the probability that he will get a yellow marble on the first try? **8/37**

What is the probability that he will pull out a yellow marble on the second try (with one marble already removed)? **8/36**

4. How many triangles are shown? **5**

How many right angles are there? **4**

How many obtuse angles are there? **1**

How many acute angles are there? **6**

5. What kind of lines are these?
○ A. perpendicular
○ B. lines
○ C. intersecting lines
● D. parallel

6. Which factors represent $3^2 × 2^2 × 5$?
○ A. 6 × 9 × 5
○ B. 3 × 2 × 2 × 2 × 5
● C. 3 × 3 × 3 × 2 × 2 × 2 × 5
○ D. 6 × 5

7. Multiply.
1,238.83 × ... = **4955.32**   799.93 × ... = **7199.30**

page 56

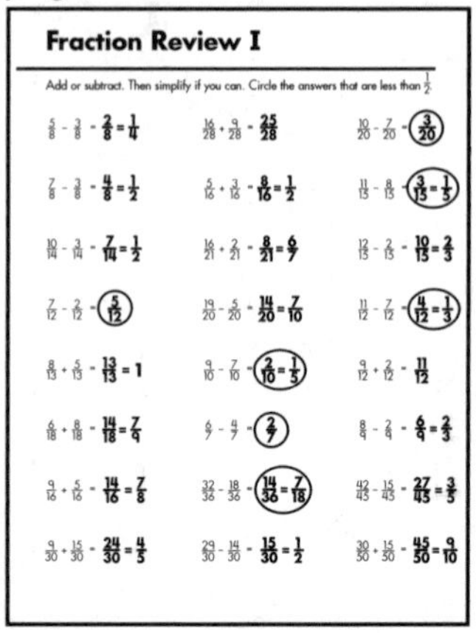

Fraction Review I

Add or subtract. Then simplify if you can. Circle the answers that are less than ½.

(fraction answers) ... ⟨circled: 3/20, 1/3, 1/6, 11/12⟩

page 57

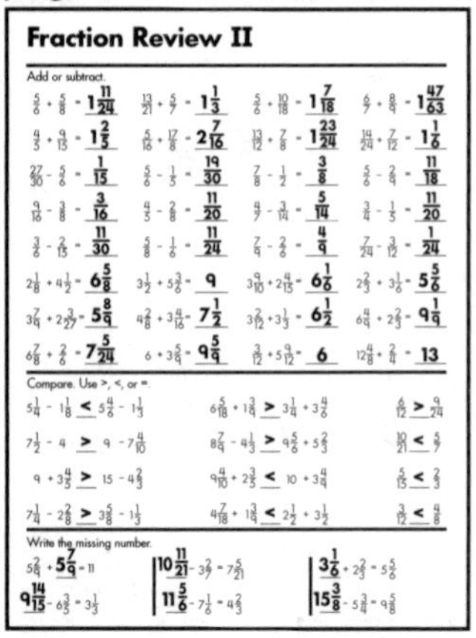

Fraction Review II

Add or subtract.

Compare. Use >, <, or =.

Write the missing number.

page 58

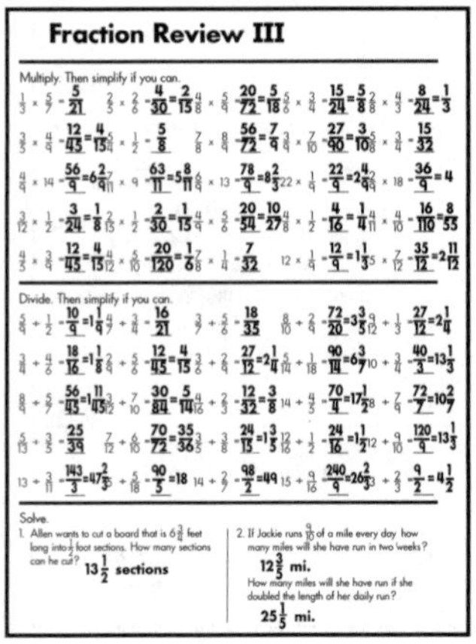

Fraction Review III

Multiply. Then simplify if you can.

Divide. Then simplify if you can.

Solve.

1. Allen wants to cut a board that is 6⅔ feet long into ½-foot sections. How many sections can he cut? **13½ sections**

2. If Jackie runs ¾ of a mile every day how many miles will she have run in two weeks? **12¼ mi.**

How many miles will she have run if she doubled the length of her daily run? **25½ mi.**

page 59

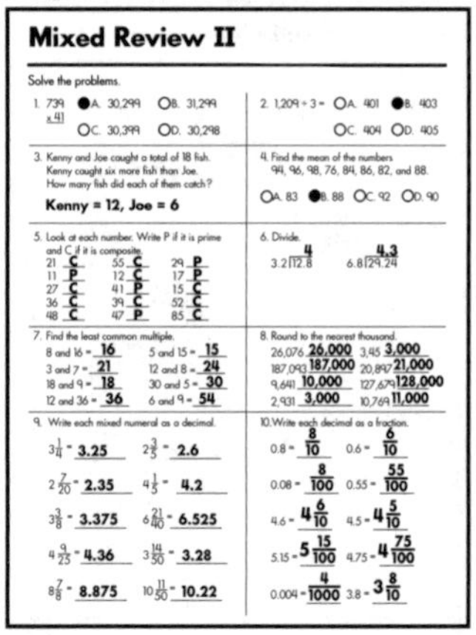

Mixed Review II

Solve the problems.

1. 7.94 × 41
○ A. 30.299   ● B. 31.299   ○ C. 30.399   ○ D. 30.298

2. 1,209 ÷ 3
○ A. 401   ● B. 403   ○ C. 404   ○ D. 405

3. Kenny and Joe caught a total of 18 fish. Kenny caught six more fish than Joe. How many fish did each of them catch? **Kenny = 12, Joe = 6**

4. Find the mean of the numbers 94, 98, 76, 84, 86, 82, and 88.
○ A. 83   ● B. 88   ○ C. 92   ○ D. 96

5. Look at each number. Write P if it is prime and C if it is composite.
21 **C**   55 **C**   29 **P**
2 **P**   21 **C**   12 **C**
11 **P**   9 **C**   30 **C**
48 **C**   67 **P**   18 **C**

6. Divide.
3.2)12.8 = **4.3**   6.87)24.74 = ...

7. Find the least common multiple.
8 and 16 **16**   5 and 15 **15**
3 and 7 **21**   12 and 8 **24**
18 and 9 **18**   30 and 5 **30**
12 and 36 **36**   7 and 14 **14**

8. Round to the nearest thousand.
26,076 → **26,000**   3,145 → **3,000**
187,694 → **187,000**   20,845 → **21,000**
9,641 → **10,000**   127,674 → **128,000**
10,976 → **11,000**

9. Write each mixed numeral as a decimal.
1 ¼ **3.25**   4¼ **4.2**
2 ⅜ **2.35**   3½ **4.5**
3 ⅜ **3.375**   6½ **6.525**
4⅓ **4.36**   3¼ **3.28**
8⅞ **8.875**   10 2/9 **10.22**

10. Write each decimal as a fraction.
0.08 = **8/100**   0.55 = **55/100**
4.6 = **46/10**   5.5 = **55/100**
4.75 = **475/100**
0.004 = **4/1000**   3.8 = **38/10**

page 60

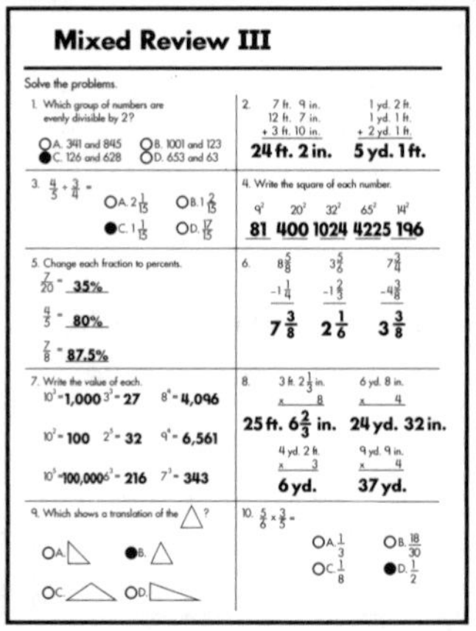

Mixed Review III

Solve the problems.

1. Which group of numbers are evenly divisible by 2?
○ A. 341 and 845   ○ B. 1001 and 123
● C. 126 and 628   ○ D. 653 and 643

2. 7 ft. 6 in. + 3 ft. 10 in.   1 yd. 2 ft. + 2 yd. 1 ft.
24 ft. 2 in.   5 yd. 1 ft.

4. Write the square of each number.
9² 20² 32² 65² 14²
81 400 1024 4225 196

5. Change each fraction to percents.
7/20 **35%**   4/5 **80%**   7/8 **87.5%**

6. 8⅜ + 7⅞ = **7⅜**   2⅛ = **3⅜**

7. Write the value of each.
$10^3 =$ **1,000** $2^3 × 27 =$ **4,096**   3 ft. 2⅓ in.   6 yd. 8 in.
$10^2 =$ **100** $2^7 × 32 =$ **6,561**   **25 ft. 6⅔ in.   24 yd. 32 in.**
$10^5 =$ **100,000** $6^3 =$ **216**   7⅛ × 3 **4 yd. 2 h.   9 yd. 4 in.**   **6 yd.   37 yd.**

9. Which shows a translation of the △?
○ A. △   ○ B. (shape)
○ C. △   ● (shape)   ○ A. 1/4   ○ B. 8/1   ○ C. 3/8   ● 1/2